THE BEST OF **WOODWORKER'S JOURNAL**

Heirloom Furniture Projects

Timeless Pieces for Your Home

from the editors of *Woodworker's Journal*

Fox Chapel Publishing

1970 Broad Street • East Petersburg, PA 17520
www.FoxChapelPublishing.com

Compilation Copyright © 2008 by Fox Chapel Publishing, Inc.

Text and illustration Copyright © 2007 by Woodworker's Journal. Woodworker's Journal is a publication of Rockler Press.

Heirloom Furniture Classic projects including doors, cabinets, chests, and tables is a compilation first published in 2008 by Fox Chapel Publishing, Inc. The patterns contained herein are copyrighted by Woodworker's Journal.

Our friends at Rockler Woodworking and Hardware supplied us with most of the hardware used in this book. Visit rockler.com. For subscription information to Woodworker's Journal magazine, call toll-free 800-765-4119.

Woodworker's Journal
Founder & CEO: Ann Rockler Jackson
Publisher: Larry N. Stoiaken
Editor-in-Chief: Rob Johnstone
Art Director: Jeff Jacobson
Senior Editor: Joanna Werch Takes
Field Editor: Chris Marshall
Illustrators: Jeff Jacobson, John Kelliher

ISBN 978-1-56523-364-5

Publisher's Cataloging-in-Publication Data

Heirloom furniture projects : timeless pieces for your home / from the
editors of Woodworker's journal. -- 1st ed. -- East Petersburg, PA :
Fox Chapel Publishing, c2008.

p. ; cm.
(The best of Woodworker's journal)
ISBN: 978-1-56523-364-5

1. Furniture making--Patterns. 2. Furniture making--Technique.
I. Series. II. Woodworker's journal.

TT195 .H45 2008
684.1/04--dc22   2008

To learn more about the other great books from Fox Chapel Publishing, or to find a retailer near
you, call toll-free 800-457-9112 or visit us at www.FoxChapelPublishing.com.

Printed in China
First Printing: July 2008

Note to Authors: We are always looking for talented authors to write new books in our area of woodworking,
design, and related crafts. Please send a brief letter describing your idea to Acquisition Editor,
Fox Chapel Publishing, 1970 Broad Street, East Petersburg, PA 17520.

Introduction

Building projects to the best of your ability takes time ... sometimes hundreds of hours of it. That's an ironclad truth, whether you're an old saw in the shop or still honing your woodworking skills. So, we should want the things we build to last a lifetime and hopefully get passed on to future generations. These sorts of heirloom projects can represent our highest level of dedication to the craft.

If you're ready to build a few "one-of-a-kind" projects for your family or friends, this new collection of Heirloom Projects should provide just the inspiration you need. We've collected 20 of our finest designs, created by some of the best woodworkers in the country. A few of these projects will provide an ambitious challenge, but others are actually more beautiful than they are hard to build—so there's something here for everyone.

For those keepsake or blanket collectors in your life, consider building Chris Inman's Baker's Shelf or Ian Kirby's Frame and Panel Chest. Bruce Kieffer offers a Memorial Flag Case, which could bring a loved one comfort while serving as a fitting reminder of military service. Or set your sights on Rick White's Gun Cabinet ... it will provide handsome display space for that prized collection of rifles or shotguns.

Nothing says heirloom like a reproduction piece, and we've gathered some great examples here. I suggest starting with Randy Bemont's Colonial Pewter Cupboard and the lap desk by J. Petrovich, then ramp up for John English's Harris Lebus Library Bureau by building our Roycroft-style Magazine Stand or Stephen Shepherd's graceful Demi-Lune Sofa Table. Definitely give our authentic Old-Time Icebox a try, especially if it conjures up memories of the real thing back in grandma's kitchen. You'll bring that family history back to life again.

Who says practical has to be commonplace? A project that gets daily use may well become a cherished heirloom someday. Our Arts & Crafts cherry bookcase, Shaker Vanity or Sapele Secretary Desk will be as purposeful as they are attractive in any décor. Need a place for coats and hats? Then add Brad Becker's Hexagon Hall Tree to your foyer. Every kitchen with high cabinets could benefit from John Hooper's Step Stool, and I'll bet the gardener in your life would fawn over the Gardener's Bench featured here. Speaking of betting, won't your poker buddies be impressed next game night if the chips come out in a custom-built Texas Hold-em Poker Box?

Finally, there's no time like the present to add a few new skills to your bag of woodworking tricks. Bill Hylton will show you how to build sturdy, six-panel Passage Doors using the latest router bit sets. If you've never tried steam bending, the Bentwood Carry All is a good place to start. Same goes for veneering: Rick White's Veneered Checkerboard is an excellent chance to showcase contrasting woods. Build it in a weekend using proven production veneering methods.

Time may be fleeting, but let's make the most of it on every project we build. I hope these heirlooms will provide many gratifying hours for you in the shop.

Larry N. Stoiaken, Publisher

Acknowledgments

Woodworker's Journal recently celebrated its 30th anniversary—a benchmark few magazines ever reach. I would like to acknowledge both the 300,000 woodworkers who make up our readership and Rockler Woodworking and Hardware (rockler.com), which provided most of the hardware, wood, and other products used to build the projects in this book.

Our publishing partner, Fox Chapel, did a terrific job re-presenting our material, and I am especially grateful to Alan Giagnocavo, Paul Hambke, John Kelsey, and Troy Thorne for their commitment to our content.

Larry N. Stoiaken, Publisher

Contents

48

26

Step Stool Memories

A trip down memory lane turned into a remedial course in woodworking basics .... not a bad idea for most any woodworker!

by John Hooper

"Boy, I sure miss the good old days."

I used to think this phrase was only used by old fogeys tired of young whippersnappers griping about the things they had to put up with—until I caught myself saying it to my son the other day. What brought this to mind was a discussion I was having with my son about the difference between schools of today and the schools of my youth. Today, children are learning to use the computer, and we were learning to use power tools. In the eighth grade, my favorite class was vocational agriculture, a class that was pretty important growing up in the rural mountains of Arkansas. My teacher, Mr. Powell, who reasoned that if he taught a little bit about many different vocations the child would either learn enough to take care of most minor things around a house or, if they proved especially capable at one skill, perhaps go on to a fulfilling

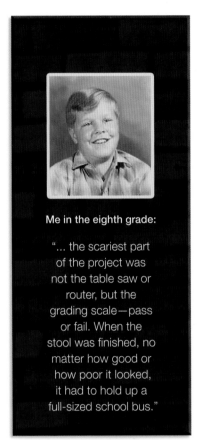

Me in the eighth grade:

"... the scariest part of the project was not the table saw or router, but the grading scale—pass or fail. When the stool was finished, no matter how good or how poor it looked, it had to hold up a full-sized school bus."

career. This single teacher had more of an impact on my life's work than all of the others combined. Woodworking, the class everyone started with, led me to many fulfilling years as a custom cabinetmaker and millwright.

The first project for all students in Mr. Powell's class was the simple step stool—except it didn't look so simple to us fledgling craftsmen. There were dadoes and weird angles and routed edges and all manner of things that we had no idea about. And the scariest part of the project was not the table saw or the router, but the grading scale—pass or fail. When the stool was finished, no matter how good or how poor the finished product looked, it had to hold up a full-sized school bus! That's impossible, we were all thinking, but Mr. Powell assured us that if we took the time and pride to do the procedures correctly, the stool would indeed stand up to the test. When the student finished, it was crunch time (hopefully not literally). The slow walk next door to the bus barn caused many

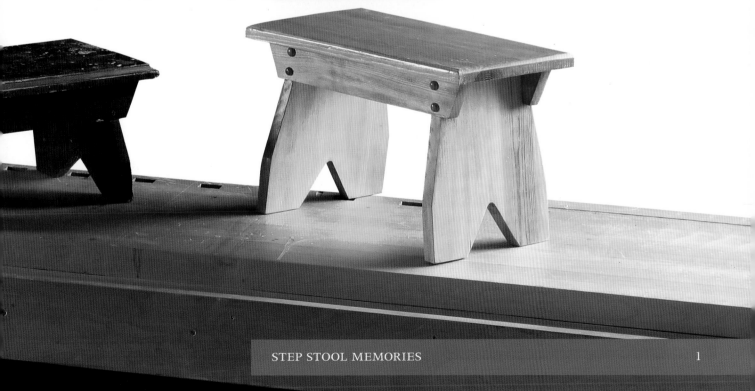

Exploded View

Step Stool
(Front View)

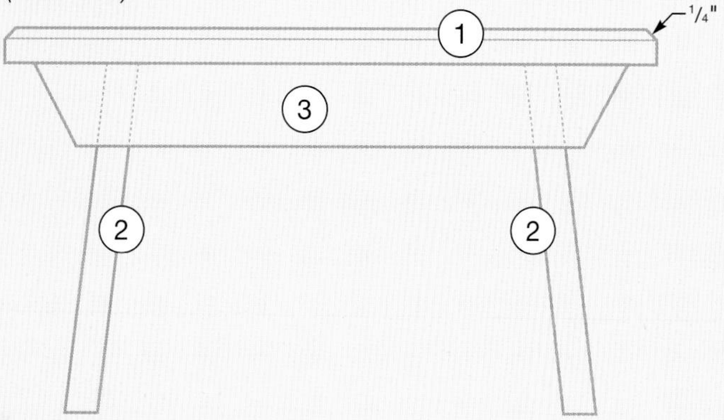
1/4"
1
3
2
2

Leg
(End View)

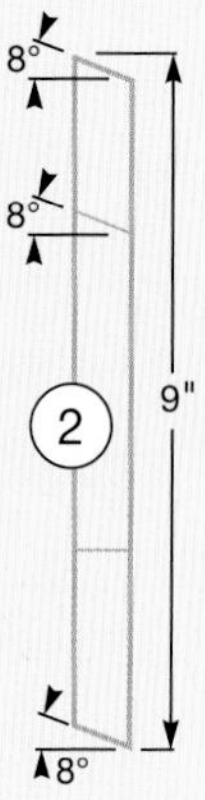
8°
8°
2
9"
8°

Leg
(Front View)

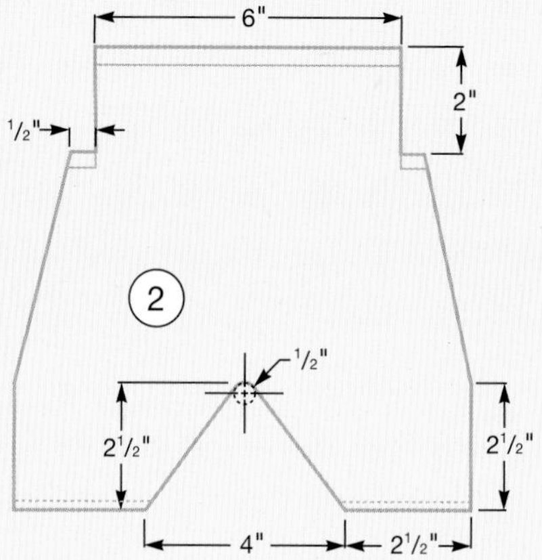
6"
2"
1/2"
2
1/2"
2 1/2"
2 1/2"
4"
2 1/2"

Stretcher
(Front and Top Views)

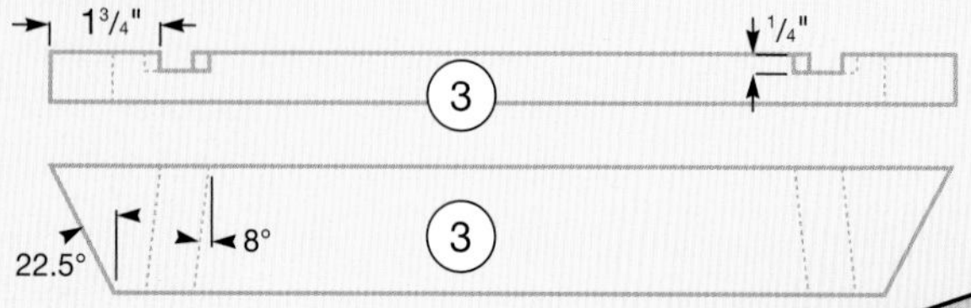
1 3/4"
1/4"
3
22.5°
8°
3

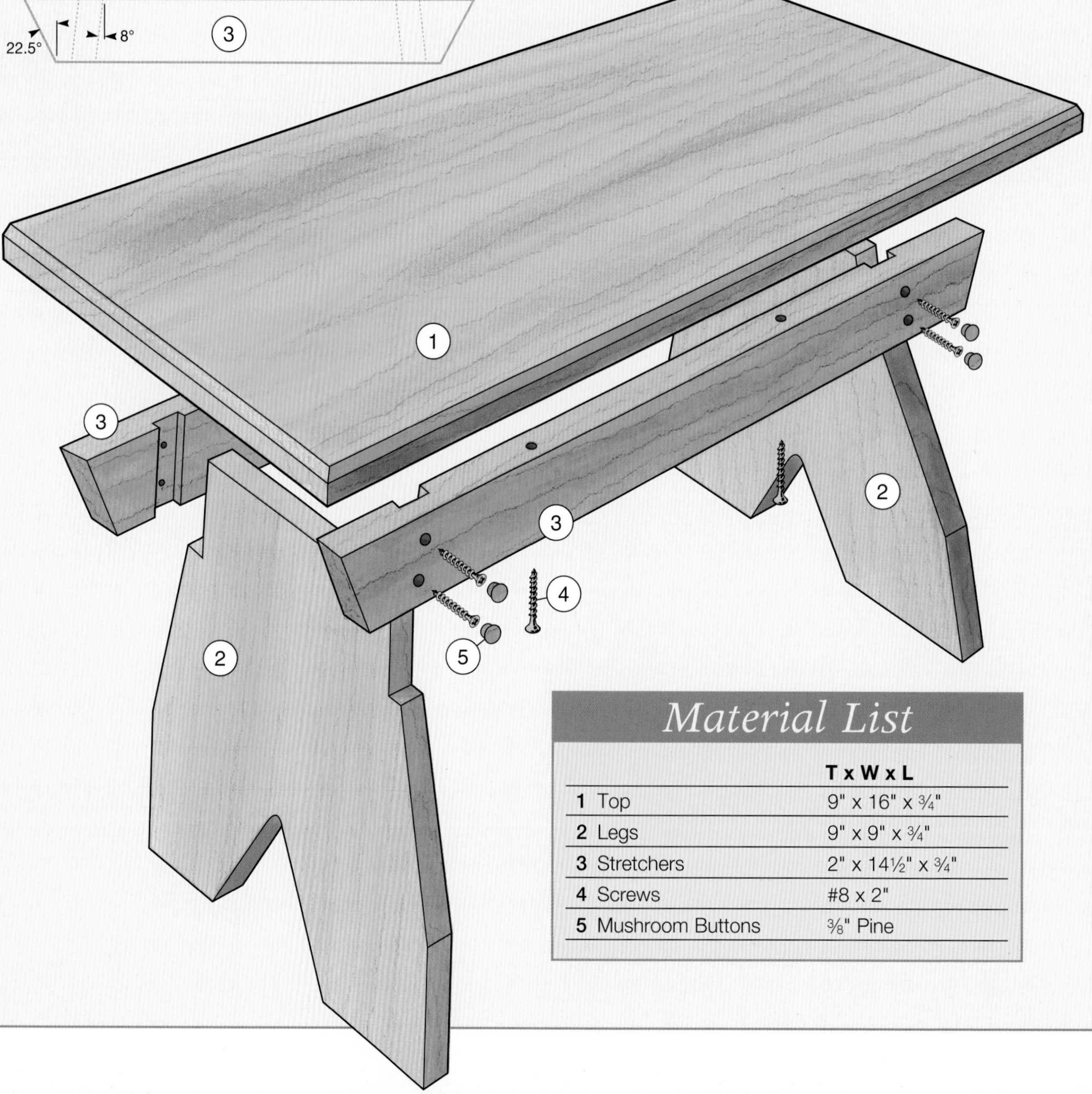
1
3
2
3
4
5
2

Material List

	T x W x L
1 Top	9" x 16" x ¾"
2 Legs	9" x 9" x ¾"
3 Stretchers	2" x 14½" x ¾"
4 Screws	#8 x 2"
5 Mushroom Buttons	⅜" Pine

of us some anxious moments. And the whole class would pour out to see the triumph or the destruction! One rear tire would be jacked up high enough for the stool to be slipped under the tires. Then the jack was let down. We were amazed at how the construction method caused a simple little wood stool to hold a full-size school bus off the ground without making a year's supply of toothpicks!

Well, 30 years later my wife came across the "little blue stool" in my dad's old barn, and when she heard the story, it became a permanent fixture in our house. No amount of coaxing convinced her I should apply a new finish—she said that old blue spray paint finish was just the perfect ambience. To me, it just looked like old spray paint. If I wanted a new finish, it looked like I was going to have to build a new stool.

A Trip Back in Time

As I headed for the shop, the thought hit me—why not do it again the same way it was done back in the eighth grade, with hand saws and chisels and all the old stuff that has been put aside for dado blades and biscuit jointers? I spent 10 minutes picking just the right four foot long piece of #2 shelving pine, then headed for the shop to see if I had forgotten the basics.

First, rip the board to a width of 9", which will become the two legs and the top. Next, the leftover is ripped to 2", which becomes the stretcher rails. Leave the measurements a little full so you can plane off the saw marks. Choose the best section of the 9" board and crosscut a 16" piece for the top (piece 1). The rest, rough cut to a length of 9½". With the table saw set at an 8° angle, crosscut the top and bottom of the legs (pieces 2) parallel to a finished length of 9". This angle of the legs will give the stool character and stability. The rest of the machining was done by hand, just as it was done back in the eighth grade. A good sharp backsaw and chisel works well in this softwood, if you stick with tradition. Next, find the centerline lengthwise on the two legs. On the top of the leg, measure 3" out on either side of center, giving you 6" between the stretcher notches. Cut the notches according to the Drawing on page 2, paying close

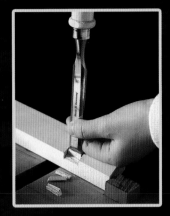

I sure hate to see those "good ol' days" slip away from our memories. Every now and then, it's kind of nice to ... do things the old way, just to show yourself you still can.

attention to the 8° angles. Then drill a ½" hole on the centerline 2½" up from the bottom. Mark the leg at the bottom 2½" away from either side and connect this mark to the ½" hole. Finish cutting out the leg as shown on the Drawing on page 2.

Next, cut the stretcher rails (pieces 3) out of the 2" piece according to the plans. Pay close attention to the 8° dadoes. A good, tight fit here makes a big difference in strength. Now the top is ready for your preference of edge treatment. I chose a simple chamfered edge done with a hand plane, but a nice Roman ogee done with a router looks just as nice. Construction can be done several ways. You can use only glue for a clean look or nails and glue, but for holding several ton automobiles off of the ground I chose plenty of glue and wood screws, just like in the old days. Only, this time, I countersunk the screws (pieces 4) and dressed up the holes with mushroom buttons (pieces 5). I used 2" screws in either end of the stretchers to attach them to the legs, then four 2" screws through the stretcher into the top. Some final sanding and your choice of finish, and you have a nice jack stand for your garage or something to help the little ones do a better job of brushing their teeth.

Well, I don't know if I won the argument with my son about which curriculum was more important; maybe computer keyboarding is more in demand these days than board straightening. But I sure hate to see "those good ol' days" slip away from our memories. Every now and then, it's kind of nice to blow the dust off of some of the old hand tools and do things the old way, just to show yourself you still can.

After getting a few pointers from her dad Allen (that's him on the first page), 7th grader Heather Manz was ready to tackle my step stool project.

Memorial Flag Case

Those bottom corners may look impossible, but a simple
tenoning jig and table saw setup make the work easy.

by Bruce Kieffer

It's tradition to drape an American flag over the casket of
a deceased U.S. forces veteran. Prior to burial, the flag is
removed, folded into a triangle and presented, "on behalf
of a grateful Nation," to the deceased veteran's next of kin.
I know this first hand because my
father recently passed away, and
our family was given his burial flag.
My mother asked me to make her
"a really nice case" for Dad's flag. I
responded without hesitation: "I'd
be honored." And even though this
is an easy thing to build, I still put my
heart into making it perfect, knowing
how proud my father would have
been with the results.

When my brother got wind
of my making Dad's flag case, he
asked if I would make one for his
father-in-law's flag as well. So I
made two out of walnut, and I used
one board for each case. I ended up
with one case having all dark and
figured wood, and the other having
all lighter, straight-grained wood.
Both are beautiful!

Getting the Fit Right
I did a little research and found out
that these flags are called burial
or interment flags. When open,
they measure 5' x 9½'. When
folded, the height from the bottom
center to the peak is approximately
10½", and the length across the
bottom is twice the height, thus 21"
long. Those were also the inside
dimensions given for "store-bought"
cases. My flags seemed a bit larger

*Using a band saw (top photo), trim away most of
the 22½° mitered joint waste. Then make the finished
cuts using a table saw and tenoning jig. Rough cutting
the joints first eliminates the risk of creating nasty
flying projectiles.*

than that, so I made a quick hot-glued-together mockup to
assure myself of the fit. I didn't bother with the 22½° mitered
ends yet; instead, I just 45° mitered the bottom ends of the
sides and set them butt on a square-cut bottom.

My flags fit really snug in
the mockup, so I made another,
this time ½" taller. To my surprise,
that was too big! One more
mockup, this time just ¼" taller
than the first, and fit was perfect.
The final inside dimensions of my
flag case became 21½" across
the bottom, with a 10¾" peak.

Cutting The Steep 22½° Miters
In the meantime, while I was
making my mockups, I'm
thinking to myself… "How the
heck am I going to cut those
steep bottom miters?" After
much experimentation, the
solution hit me. If I set my table
saw blade to 22½°, and hold
the workpieces upright, I can
cut the angle I need. Now,
what better tool is there to
hold the pieces upright other
than a tenoning jig! I tested
the setup, and it worked great.
The only drawback was that
with my saw blade raised to
its maximum of 3", the widest
front molding I could cut was
1⅛". You'll need to check your
maximum blade height and
shrink the width of your front
moldings as needed.

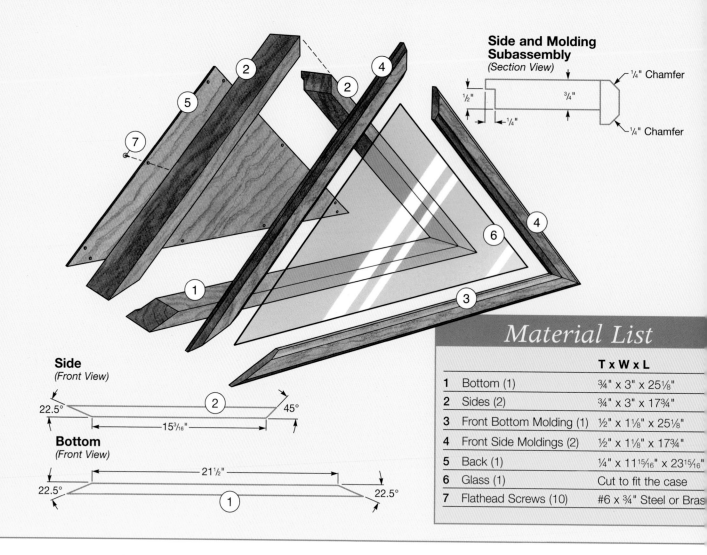

Side and Molding Subassembly
(Section View)

¼" Chamfer
½"
¾"
¼"
¼" Chamfer

Side
(Front View)

22.5° ② 45°
15³⁄₁₆"

Bottom
(Front View)

21½"
22.5° ① 22.5°

Material List

		T x W x L
1	Bottom (1)	¾" x 3" x 25⅛"
2	Sides (2)	¾" x 3" x 17¾"
3	Front Bottom Molding (1)	½" x 1⅛" x 25⅛"
4	Front Side Moldings (2)	½" x 1⅛" x 17¾"
5	Back (1)	¼" x 11¹⁵⁄₁₆" x 23¹⁵⁄₁₆"
6	Glass (1)	Cut to fit the case
7	Flathead Screws (10)	#6 x ¾" Steel or Bras

Build the Main Case

The main case consists of the bottom (piece 1) and the sides (pieces 2). Cut the sides to the dimensions given in the Materials List, adding one inch to the length. Using a miter saw, cut the top corner 45° mitered ends, then cut the sides to their finished lengths. Cut the bottom to its finished size. Set a bevel square to 22½° and mark the bottom to side joints. Remove most of the waste with your band saw.

Now for the tenoning jig and table saw setup. Make sure your tenoning jig table and fence are aligned 90° to your saw's table, and that the saw's blade is tilted to 22½°. As you can see in the photo on the previous page, I placed a ¾" thick spacer between the work piece and the tenoning jig's table to keep the saw blade far away from the jig, and I screwed a backer board to the tenoning jig's fence to reduce tearout at the rear of the cuts. I

Rout the back rabbets on the sides and bottom. Do this procedure by making several passes, slowly increasing the depth of each cut. This will reduce the chance of tearout.

used a ⅛" thick riser board, which rests on the saw's table behind the blade and to the side of the tenoning jig. When you clamp your workpieces in the tenoningjig, you do so with them on top of the riser board, so the jig holds everything ⅛" off of the saw's table, and the wood can't bind against the table as you saw.

Use scrap wood to test your table saw setup. Adjust the blade to tenoning jig distance so the cut makes a point on the end of the workpiece without reducing its length. Cut the ends of two scraps and check the combined angle to verify that it's exactly 45°. Make any necessary adjustments, then finish cut the 22½° miters.

Rout the rabbets for the back on the rear edges of the sides and bottom and then clamp the main case pieces together using band clamps. Make sure the top edges are flush at the corners.

Band clamps are a fast and sure way to clamp together the bottom and sides of this complex shape. Place pieces of cardboard under the bands at the corner joints to keep the glue from smearing and the bands from binding.

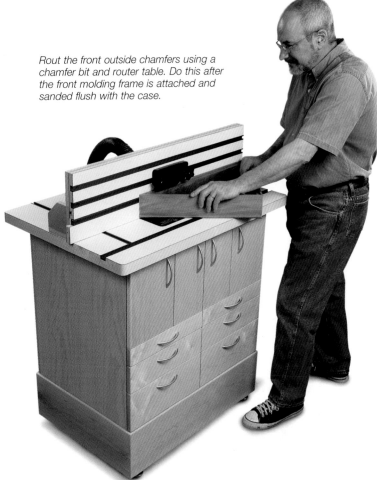

Rout the front outside chamfers using a chamfer bit and router table. Do this after the front molding frame is attached and sanded flush with the case.

Make the Front Molding Frame

Make the front moldings (pieces 3 and 4) the same way you made the case sides and bottom. Cut the moldings 1⁄32" longer, so when attached to the main case, their edges will overhang slightly. Covering the molding end faces with masking tape prior to cutting the 22½° miters greatly reduces tearout.

Use a router table and chamfer bit to rout the molding inside chamfers. Finish sand the chamfers and inside edges. Glue and band clamp the moldings together to make the frame. After that cures, glue and clamp the frame to the main case.

Do the Finish Work

You're just about done ... but there are a few more steps. Start by sanding the frame edges flush with the main case. Next, rout the frame outside chamfers and complete your finish sanding of the whole case. The final construction step is to make the back (piece 5), testing the fit as you go, to ensure a nice, tight fit. Finally, finish the case with three coats of clear stain spray lacquer. Take the case to your local glass supplier and have them fit the glass (piece 6). Set the glass in the case and affix it with a few dollops of clear silicon or hot glue. Add protective felt dots to the bottom, insert your flag, and attach the back. I can tell you right now, once you build one, there are probably a couple more in your future!

Adjusting Dimensions for Flag Sizes

While it's true that interment flags are all the same size, there are plenty of folks out there with a flag that isn't flying anymore, but still has some special meaning to a family. Rather than fold it up in a box, a flag case like the one built here can become the perfect honored resting place for a treasured family heirloom.

The Elevation Drawing at right shows you the formula to use to decide on your box dimensions. Remember, start with scrap wood and test the fit of your folded flag.

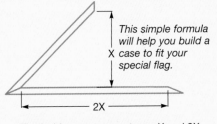

This simple formula will help you build a case to fit your special flag.

The inside measurements are X and 2X (e.g. if X =10¼", then 2X = 20½")

A Hexagon Hall Tree

Beautiful and valuable projects do not have to take months to build. This lovely hall tree combines walnut and maple construction with iron-forged hooks to create an heirloom piece in a weekend.

by Brad Becker

When guests arrive at your home does the nearest bed suddenly fill up with coats and hats? You're not alone. Whether you're young or old, live in the North or South, own your home or rent, there's rarely a good place for visitors' outerwear. And hall trees from the local furniture store always seem to be an afterthought ... lightweight, without style, and uniformly chocolate brown ... not suitable for a real woodworker's home.

So when Rob Johnstone and Jeff Jacobson (the Woodworker's Journal project gurus) came to me and said they had a good idea for a hall tree project, I didn't yawn ... but I wasn't expecting to be impressed either. I should have known they had something up their sleeves.

"When is an inlay not an inlay?" they asked. (I get paid to do woodworking, but I have to put up with this sort of silliness, because I work with editors and art directors.)

"I give ... when is an inlay not inlay?" I responded.

"When it lies next to an inlay!" they exclaimed.

Something in the look on my face must have told them I was still waiting for a punchline, because they quickly showed me their drawings. And, I had to admit, it was a great idea and a lovely design, despite the silly riddle.

Reverse Inlay

In truth, there is no such thing as a reverse inlay, but the visual effect achieved on our hexagon column lends itself to that description. By gluing thin and comparatively wide strips of walnut into the center of each facet of the hexagon,

Trick of the Eye: Reverse Inlay

The hall tree looks as if it is made from solid walnut, but the core is hard maple, exposed only at the corners to create the illusion that the maple is inlaid.

Column with Walnut Inlays

3"

1/8"

1/8"

1 1/8"

30°

1

2

Column Subassembly
(End View)

the exposed maple appears to be the inlayed piece, not the walnut. That, in a nutshell, was the fresh idea Rob and Jeff brought to this project. They also asked me to glue up the legs with two ½" laminations of walnut. They wanted the legs to have a shapely profile, but were concerned about the narrow "ankles." I added the simple lamination approach to offset the weakness in the problematic "short grain" area.

Starting with the Column

Although the general impression of this hall tree is one of elegance and quality, it is, at its heart, a very simple project. A long weekend will be all the time you'll need to put it together. (That, and another day or two to allow your finish to completely cure.)

Begin by creating the column (piece 1) by cutting a solid piece of light colored lumber. We used hard maple, and milled it to the dimensions found on the Material List on page 11. Because I had it on hand, I used a piece of stock that was not glued up. But it would not be a problem, in fact

Dead-on Layout is the Key to Success

there would be a couple of advantages, if you wanted to laminate your column from a few pieces of thinner material. If you go that route, just take an extra minute or two during the next step to keep the glue joints from bisecting one of the hexagon's corners. Your tree will look a lot better if you avoid that situation. Now take the column and mark the ends with pencil lines set at 30° from each face to form a hexagon. Take your time with this step. Each facet has to be of equal width for the reverse inlay technique to work properly. I recommend adding a few inches of extra column material so you can trim off the end of your stock, mark the cutoff and use it to get a perfectly setup saw In fact, you might even make a short test blank if you don't have some drop-stock to work with. Once you have the end marked, step to your table saw, angle the blade to exactly 30°, and set the height. If your table saw is a traditional right-tilt version, you will need to move your fence to the left of the saw blade, as shown in the photo below. Carefully align the saw blade to the layout line on your test blank (or your actual column, if you are either brave or foolish) by adjusting the fence. Make the first slice along the length of the piece, then flip the piece end-for-end and position your stock so you are cutting the adjoining facet of the hexagon (you will create a point or corner, as shown in

The two-step plowing technique for the grooves in the hexagon is a sure way to keep the opening in the exact center of each facet.

the photo below). Measure the two facets to see if they are equal. Adjust the fence if they are not and try the operation again. Once the setup is correct, you can start on the actual column stock. It's best to set up a featherboard (exactly in the center of the width of the column) to add an element of control and safety.

Plowing the Facet Grooves

With your freshly formed hexagon in hand, move to your router table to plow the grooves in each facet. I'd grab that test blank you made as well, to once again assist in setting up a proper cut.

I used a two-step plowing technique to center the grooves in the column's facets. I set a ⅝" straight bit to a depth of ⅛". Look to the Drawings on page 13 to find the exact dimensions for the grooves. Verify your setup by using the test blank. Once all is well, go ahead and plow the facet grooves.

Moving back to the table saw, I ripped ⅛" thick walnut strips (pieces 2) to fill the void created by the facet grooves. Before ripping the pieces, take a bit of time to select the best looking stock for this task.

Fit the walnut strips to the grooves and get ready for glue-up. Because it works so well with walnut, I used Titebond® dark wood glue for this assembly. I glued and clamped two facets per session and had the walnut in place in short order. While you're gluing and clamping the column, you can start on to the legs in your down time.

The author demonstrates how to form the hexagon column of hall tree. The featherboard is removed in this photo clarity, but the author highly recommends usin properly placed featherboard added safe

Hall Tree Project Supplies

The following supplies are available from Woodworker's Journal.

Hook* #23136
Dovetail Bit #91023
*Three required.
To order your supplies, call 800-610-0883 and mention code W5043.

Cap Base and Crown Detail
(Top and Side Views)

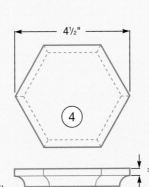

6"

4½"

⑤

④

Cove bit

³⁄₈"

Each square equals ½"

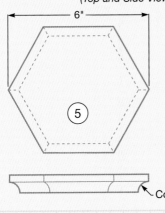

Builder's Tip:
Use a photocopier to enlarge this drawing 400%. Then make your leg pattern from the full-size copy.

Leg

NOTE: *Mount the hall tree's hooks on the same facets as the legs to ensure stability.*

Hall Tree

⑤
④

⑥

Column Construction Glue-up Detail
(Top View)

Corner

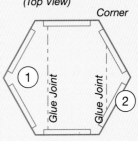

① Glue Joint

② Glue Joint

If you choose to glue up your column from more than one piece of wood, make sure the glue joints will not bisect the hexagon's corners.

②
①

③

Material List

	T x W x L
1 Column (1)	3" x 3" x 66"
2 Walnut Strips* (6)	⅛" x 1⅛" x 66"
3 Leg Blanks** (6)	½" x 5" x 16½"
4 Cap Base (1)	¾" x 4½" x 4½"
5 Cap Crown (1)	¾" x 6" x 6"
6 Hooks (3)	Forged iron

*Trim to final width after you make the facet-grooves.
**Glued together in pairs to create three legs.*

Laminated Legs Will Never Fail You

Because there are six sides to the hall tree, it is incredibly simple to attach three legs to the column. As you know, three-legged stools, tables or even hall trees have the advantage of never needing to be leveled.

Although there are only three legs, I used six pieces of wood to make them; as I said earlier, it makes them much stronger. Cut the leg laminations (pieces 3) from ½" walnut stock. For appearance's sake, try to make each leg from stock that matches well. (I cut each pair of leg laminations from the same board.) Glue the blanks together, making 1" thick leg stock. With the aid of the Gridded Drawing on page 12, make a pattern of the leg shape. If you are not familiar with using gridded drawings, you have a couple of options. The first is to create a grid of ½" squares on sturdy paper. Draw matching lines on your grid to the ones in the Gridded Drawing. This will provide a very close representation of the leg shape. Don't be afraid to refine the shape as you see fit. The second option is to use a copier to enlarge the gridded drawing by 400%.

The author used a spindle sander to complete the shaping of the legs and to remove any saw marks from the leg's edges.

Once you have your pattern, transfer the shape to each leg blank and use a band saw to cut them out. (Keep the drop stock: you'll use it to set up your router table later.) I used a spindle sander to complete the shaping of the legs and smooth out any saw marks left behind.

Go back to the column that you've completed gluing the walnut strips into. Scrape off any glue squeeze-out and then use a belt sander or good sized disc sander to clean up the facets and sand them smooth. Be careful not to round over the flat aspect of each facet. Now you're ready to do some dovetailing.

Sliding Home

The legs are attached to the column with sliding dovetails, which are easier to make than you may think. (You could, of course, use a more basic mortise and tenon joint ... it would hold up fine, but where's the fun in that?)

Chuck a ½" 14° dovetail bit into your router table and set its depth to $\frac{5}{16}$" deep. You are going to plow the column dovetail grooves $3\frac{5}{8}$" long, exactly in the center of the facets. Set up a stop on your fence to register each cut perfectly. Plow all three grooves and then grab your legs ... the hall tree legs.

This is where the drop stock that you saved when band sawing the legs comes in handy. You need to set the fence of your router table to cut the matching dovetails on the legs. Get the setup close and then use the drop stock to test the cut. Make one pass down each side of the stock as shown in the photo on page 13. The joint should slide into the groove in the leg with just a hint of resistance. Once you've got the table adjusted correctly, form the dovetails on the back of each leg. Now all you need to do is trim the dovetail (down from the top edge of the leg) so it matches the length

E-mail has mostly eliminated good old-fashioned letters, but you still have to pay bills and send those birthday cards. Here's a project that will allow you to do so in comfort!

I chose cherry for this project, because it has a soft, tactile look to it and lovely coloration. Because this desk is made from thin stock, you'll probably need to plane ¾" material down to size. Be certain to remove equal amounts of wood from both faces of the boards to reduce the chance of cupping. Or, use quartersawn lumber instead, especially for the wide top and bottom panels, which are especially prone to warp.

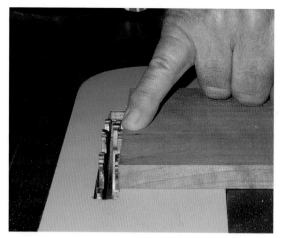

When laying out your box joints (see box below), the first step is to set your dado blade height ¹⁄₃₂" higher than the thickness of the stock.

Assembling the Desk Box

Start construction by cutting the sides (pieces 1), front and back (pieces 2) to size. Dovetails would provide a traditional look for this box, but box joints are easier to construct, equally attractive, and plenty strong. Plus, you can make them entirely on the table saw.

You'll need to build a very simple box joint jig for your saw's miter gauge, similar to the one shown in the sidebar below. Make the jig's backer board from a piece of hardwood scrap,

approximately 6" x 12". Glue a ½" x ½" x 2" registration peg into a slot in the backer board. Clamp the jig to your miter gauge and make some test cuts on matching scrap to fine-tune its setting. When your test cuts produce joints that mesh with an easy friction fit, cut the actual corner joints on the box parts.

Gluing Up the Corner Joints

Scrape or sand the faces of the boards to 220 grit. Be careful not to round over the edges of the joint pins. Spread glue onto the contact surfaces of the joints with an artist's palette knife or small paintbrush to help minimize glue squeeze-out. Try to keep glue out of the inside corners where it's tough to clean up. Clamp the box together and check it for square.

Separating the Halves

When the glue cures, pare the faces of the corner joints and the edges of the box flush, using a low-angle block plane set for a thin cut. You're now ready to split the box in two. The perfect tool would be a large, well-tuned bandsaw, but most of us don't have a bandsaw of sufficient size. The next best choice is the table saw.

First, lay out the two angled cuts on the sides of the box (see the Drawings on page 25). If you are following these plans exactly, the angle should be 7°. Tilt your saw blade to this angle and adjust the rip fence to width. Raise the blade to about 1½" and make the first angled rip cut. Readjust the fence to width before cutting the opposite side of the box. This will leave about 7" of material left to cut on the

Five Steps to Cutting Perfect Box Joints On Your Table Saw

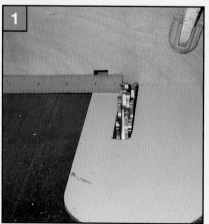

To set up the box joint jig, mount a ½"-wide dado blade in your saw and raise the blade to the thickness of the box sides plus ¹⁄₃₂". This will create joint pins that protrude slightly. Clamp the jig to the miter gauge so at least 3" extends to the right of the blade and cut your first slot for the jig's registration peg.

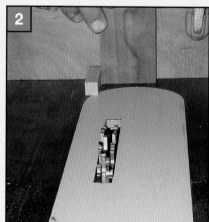

Next, loosen the clamp and adjust the jig so it's exactly one slot width away from the first slot (see Fig. 1) and cut your second slot. Measure carefully: Precision is critical here. Make the registration peg from hardwood and glue it into the first slot. To use the jig, hold a test piece firmly against

sides. Use a Japanese-style handsaw to complete these two cuts (see photo at right). After the lid and base are separated, smooth the sawn edges with a block plane to create an even fit all around.

Mortising the Hardware

Letting in the hinges and lockset requires time and patience. Chisel the mortises by hand in the following sequence: 1) strap hinges; 2) lock and link; and 3) writing board hinges. The strap hinges should be located and marked with the two halves butted against one another. The writing board hinges must be offset from one another to allow for passage and closure. They must also be counter-mortised where the knuckles of the hinges meet the opposing box half. A small, sharp gouge works well for this job. The last bit of chisel work is to let in some depressions that allow access so you can easily lift the writing boards. Once the chiseling is completed, install the hardware.

Use a table saw blade tipped to 7° to begin the process of separating the box lid from the base, then switch to a handsaw to complete the cuts on the sides.

Making the Writing Boards

A writing surface should be smooth and durable. I recommend using ¼" "Baltic" or "Finnish" birch plywood for the writing boards (pieces 3). It has five "plys," no voids and usually is without "blow holes" on its faces. The tight, even laminations of the material hold screws well, and the grain usually requires no filling. Cut the boards to allow ¹⁄₁₆" of reveal between the box sides and the edges of the boards. Next, form the angled mortises (see drawings) for the hinges into these boards with a sharp chisel. Fasten the board hinges in place.

With the boards hinged, locate the board rests (pieces 4) and glue them in place. Remember to rip the 7° angle onto the top edge of this piece. After the glue has cured, unscrew the boards from their hinges and rout or chisel in the finger depressions that allow access for lifting the writing boards.

Many of the writing boards I have seen on older desks are covered in leather or felt. An easier approach is to use the following Chinese painting and lacquering technique. Sand the boards to 180 grit and coat the faces and edges with acrylic gesso (available at art supply stores). The boards are now ready to accept color. The Chinese used shellac mixed with pigment for the next step. I use a product called "Fresco Color" instead of authentic Chinese pigment. Mix the pigment into the shellac to a consistency of about whole milk— make it slightly thicker than a 3-lb. cut.

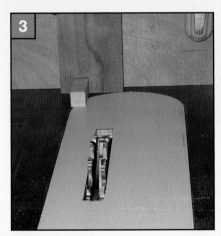

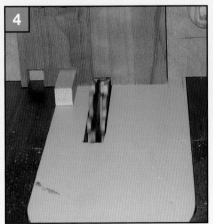

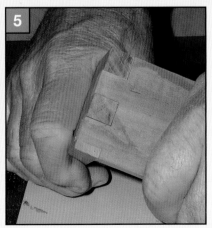

the peg, and make the first cut to create the joint's first pin and slot (see Fig. 2). Fit the slot over the jig peg and repeat the process to cut pins and slots across the test piece (see Fig. 3). Cutting the mating piece correctly involves starting with a slot instead of a pin. To do this, use the outermost pin of the first

test board as a spacer, fitting the test piece over the registration peg. Butt the second board against the first to cut the edge slot (see Fig. 4). Now mill the remaining pins and slots. Test the fit of the joint parts. They should be snug and require little more than a good push to slip together (see Fig. 5). If

they are loose, reclamp the jig slightly to the right to cut wider pins. Loosen a tight fit by shifting the jig to the left. A light tap is often all that's required to dial in the jig. Cut more test pieces to check your adjustments.

Make the escutcheon plate from $\frac{1}{16}$" thick brass. My escutcheon measures $2\frac{1}{2}$" in diameter. Use a centerpunch to locate the keyhole, then cut out the shape to your liking.

Brush the paint on quickly but carefully; it dries fast. Apply two coats, sanding lightly between them. Allow the paint to dry over night. If any final sanding is necessary, do it gently to avoid penetrating the color. Before applying the top coats of lacquer, you can add a bit of surface decoration with faux gilding. I use an ordinary gold paint pen and a black permanent marker. With my fingers serving as a marking gauge sliding against the edge of the board, I simply move the pen to draw the lines. Apply the gold first and then the black.

An alternative method of coloring the boards is to use aerosol enamel instead of shellac and pigment. Start with the gesso, then spray-paint the boards. Give the paint 24 hours to dry.

Whichever painting method you choose, topcoat the writing boards with two coats of lacquer. Normally I use gloss lacquer and adjust the sheen if necessary by rubbing out the finish. For the writing boards I was concerned about revealing the gesso, so I used a semi-gloss lacquer. If you paint with enamel, the lacquer may be incompatible with it. You will need to apply at least two sealing coats of 3-lb. shellac before lacquering.

Finally, locate the rare earth magnets. They should be situated about $\frac{1}{8}$" from either edge of the board on the side opposite the hinges. Then install simple upholstery tacks, filed neatly round and driven into the board rests, to serve as tiny contact points for the magnets.

Adding the Desk Top and Bottom

As I suggested earlier, quartersawn lumber will make the most stable top and bottom panels (pieces 5). While this may seem a little finicky and expensive, it's good insurance against cupping later on.

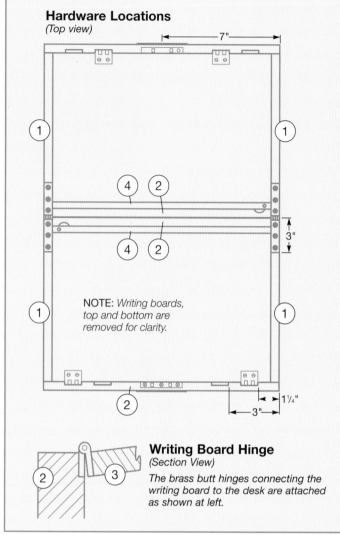

Hardware Locations
(Top view)

NOTE: *Writing boards, top and bottom are removed for clarity.*

Writing Board Hinge
(Section View)

The brass butt hinges connecting the writing board to the desk are attached as shown at left.

Edge-gluing $\frac{3}{8}$" material requires a delicate touch. First hand-plane the edges and check for squareness, then spread the glue and rub the mating edges together to ensure an even coating. Apply just enough clamping pressure to keep the boards from shifting during curing.

Glue the top and bottom panels to the desk's sides one at a time. Line up each panel so it is evenly spaced from the sides of the box and flush with the back or strap hinge side. Lightly mark the location of the sides on the top and bottom with a few dots. Apply glue to the box side of the joint, not to the top or bottom. Be judicious. Too much glue will produce squeeze-out that will be difficult to clean up. Scrape off the excess in an hour or two.

Finishing Up with a Handmade Escutcheon Plate

To finish the desk I applied one coat of Watco's Danish oil and allowed it to dry for three days. I applied the oil only

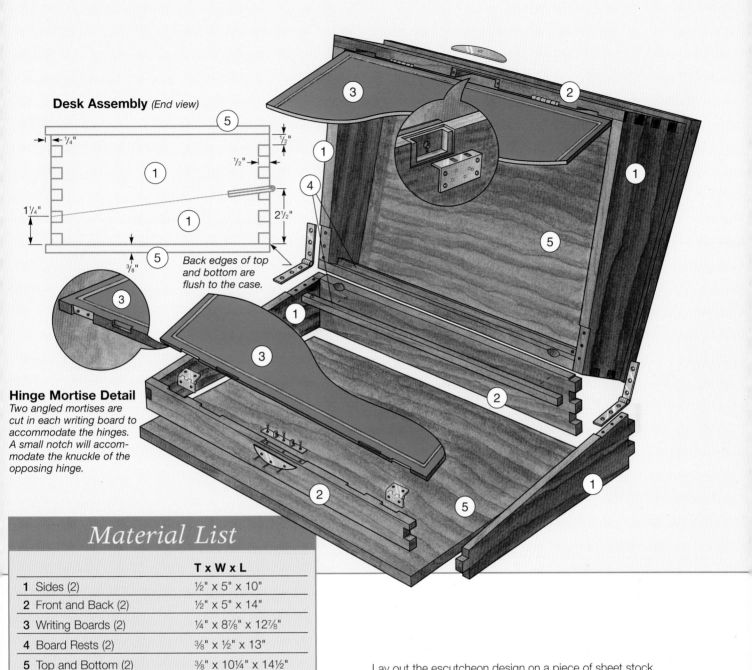

Desk Assembly *(End view)*

¼"

½"

½"

1¼"

2½"

⅜"

Back edges of top and bottom are flush to the case.

Hinge Mortise Detail
Two angled mortises are cut in each writing board to accommodate the hinges. A small notch will accommodate the knuckle of the opposing hinge.

Material List

		T x W x L
1	Sides (2)	½" x 5" x 10"
2	Front and Back (2)	½" x 5" x 14"
3	Writing Boards (2)	¼" x 8⅞" x 12⅞"
4	Board Rests (2)	⅜" x ½" x 13"
5	Top and Bottom (2)	⅜" x 10¼" x 14½"

to the outside and the edges of the desk's interior. I then sprayed a single coat of gloss lacquer on the interior and used 400-grit sandpaper to smooth it. The exterior received three light coats of semi-gloss lacquer, with a light sanding between coats.

The last step in construction is to install an escutcheon plate. Escutcheon plates are readily available from most hardware suppliers, but I was after something different. I tried to imagine what the box will look like in a few years: a deep red color with little obvious grain. I wanted the escutcheon to accentuate the box, so I made it from a disc of ¹⁄₁₆"-thick brass. If you'd like to do the same, here's how to make it:

Lay out the escutcheon design on a piece of sheet stock. Locate the keyhole and centerpunch it for drilling. Drill out the keyhole, then cut out the shape. Refine the shape of the plate and the keyhole with files. Ease the edges by filing a tiny bevel all around. You can planish the surface if you like with an 8- to 12-ounce ball peen hammer, working lightly. To color the brass, I used several applications of Brass Black (available at gun stores) that I buffed selectively. The bit of "antiquing," produced by the Brass Black, serves to accent the planishing marks and minor scratches. Install the escutcheon with several tiny brass brads.

Now, fill it with stationery and enjoy your new "laptop." Whether you're journaling, penning letters or writing the next great thriller, this desk should age gracefully and serve you well.

Dovetail keys and beautiful brass hardware add a touch of sophistication to this easy to assemble weekend project.

Texas Hold 'Em Poker Box

The Texas Hold 'em version of the quintessential American card game has swept the nation, intriguing princes and paupers alike. Here's a classic poker chip box, featuring keyed dovetails, flush brass hardware, and even a secret compartment!

by Brad Becker

I became interested in Texas Hold 'em after watching some celebrities play it on television. While I'm not really a gambler, this seemed to be a game you could enjoy if you were playing for money or just for chips. After playing it for a spell, I was inspired to make a nice box to hold the chips, cards, and maybe even a little secret poker cash. The hardware I used for this project is a real key to the design, and it's available to readers (see *Hard-to-find Hardware* box inside).

I had some nice ½"-thick mahogany lumber that I'd been saving for just the right project. I also used solid brass hardware, because it looks great with stain-enhanced mahogany. After a few simple tests to be sure the hardware would work for this project, I milled up my lumber.

Starting with the Front, Back and Ends

Select your best-looking stock, and set aside a really nice piece for the lid panel before you slice blanks for the front, back and ends (pieces 1, 2, and 3) on your table saw. (Note that the front is ³⁄₁₆" wider than the other three pieces.) Before mitering the ends of these box parts, lay out the drawer opening in the front. I made the drawer face (piece 4) using a cutout from the box front, in order to keep the grain flowing nicely across the box front. Mark out the

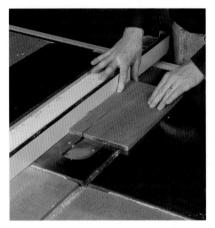
Rip the front piece into three strips with a thin-kerfed blade in the table saw. The middle strip becomes the drawer face.

drawer opening on the front panel (see the Drawings in the foldout section).

Cutting the Drawer Face

Using a thin-kerf blade in your table saw, make two long rips down the length of the front, to remove the drawer face (piece 4)—splitting the front into three strips. Now scribe the ends of the drawer face onto the middle strip with a marking knife. Use a Japanese saw to trim the drawer face to length. Set the drawer face aside for now. Take the four remaining pieces of the front and carefully glue them back together. By doing so you will create the drawer opening.

While the glue cures, head back to the table saw and set up for mitering the ends of the front, back and ends. Switch to a sharp, stiff blade and test

your blade tilt on some scrap MDF to make sure that you're cutting dead on at 45°. To help nail those miter cuts, I screwed a simple fence onto my miter gauge to keep the pieces from shifting during cutting. I also clamped a stop block to the fence to cut each pair of parts exactly the same length. Be sure to scrape off any dried glue squeeze-out on the box front before you miter its ends, then cut the ends of the back. Reposition and clamp your stop block, and miter the sides now, too.

Trim off the ends of the middle strip to bring the drawer face to final size. Make the cuts with a pull saw, and use a block of wood next to the blade to keep the cuts square.

While you're still at the table saw, form the groove on the inside of each piece to fit the bottom of the box later (see the Drawings for location). Then move to the router table to cut the shallow rabbets on the top inside edges of the front, back and ends that will hold the lid panel in place.

Glue the top and bottom strips of the front panel and the offcuts from the drawer front together to create the drawer opening.

Assembling the Box

Time for some assembly. First, cut the bottom (piece 5) from ⅛" plywood, then spread glue carefully on the miters, slip the bottom into its slots dry and use a couple of band clamps to hold the assembly as the glue cures. Don't forget to check the diagonal measurements to confirm it's square.

When the glue dries, slice the lid frame off the box with four successive cuts at the table saw.

With the lid frame cut free, it's time to make some mortises. The lock on the front and the lid support each need a mortise to seat properly, as do the solid brass handles on the box ends. I used an ⅛" router bit, rub collar and a shop-made hardboard templates to form the handle mortises. Next, drill the key hole and then chop the lock mortise by hand with a sharp chisel.

Trim the ends of the four box parts to 45°. Use a sled attached to the miter gauge and a stop block to control these delicate miter cuts.

To cut the mortise in the box end for the lid support, I set up my router table and plunged the box down over the bit, which worked like a charm (photo above right). Stop blocks registered the ends of the cut, and a featherboard kept the box end tight against the fence. Finally, drill a hole to accept the locking pin as shown in the Drawings on page 30.

I use a trim router and rub collar around a straight bit to template rout mortises for the lock and recessed brass box handles.

Routing Dovetail Keyways

The last bit of routing on the box involves making pairs of dovetail keyway slots in each of the boxes mitered corners. I used a shop-made dovetail key (sidebar above, far right) jig and a 14° dovetail bit in the router table to cut these mortises (See bottom photo, next column). The jig holds the box at 45° to the router table surface.

Use the same dovetail bit partially set into the router fence to mill your keys (pieces 6) to final shape. For safety reasons, form long strips when routing them (my keys are made of ebony). When the key strips fit into their dovetail mortises with just a bit of friction, cut them overly long, apply a little glue in the mortises and slide them into place. Trim and sand them flush after the glue dries.

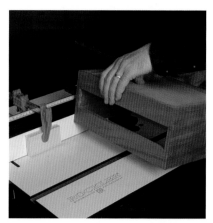

To rout the lid support mortise, plunge the box down over the bit, stopping the cut with clamped stop blocks.

Wrapping Up the Lid and Moldings

To finish up the lid construction, cut enough stock to make the lid molding (piece 7), and mill the rabbet on this molding at your router table. The rabbet will hold the lid panel (piece 8) in the frame. Cut the lid panel to size, then tip your saw blade and bevel the top face of the panel all around, supporting it by standing it up against a tall fence. Give the panel a thorough sanding. Now set the panel into the lid frame, miter cut the lid moldings to length, and glue them in place. Be sure to keep glue out of the lid panel groove. Once the glue has cured, locate and chop small mortises for the hinges. Form a tiny bevel on the back edge of the lid, this will allow the lid to open

It's easy to cut pairs of keyway mortises in the box corners with a sled-type jig that holds the box at 45° to the router table.

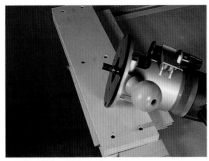

Figure 1: *Sandwich several layers of veneer between two jointed pieces of scrap plywood, then use an edge-trimming bit to establish a straight edge.*

Figure 2: *With the straight edge against your table saw fence, rip the plywood, and thus the veneers, into strips. Then joint both edges of each strip down to a 2" width.*

Figure 3: *With a fine blade installed in the table saw, crosscut the jointed strips into 2" squares, using a long auxiliary fence and a stop block.*

Making a Sandwich

Begin building the checkerboard by cutting the substrate to size (see the Material List at left), then turn your attention to the 64 squares of veneer. You can cut enough squares for up to three boards at the same time using the following method.

Select veneer that is at least 4¼" wide. On the jointer, dress one edge of each of two pieces of scrap plywood, then sandwich alternating sheets of veneer (first walnut, then maple and so on) between the pieces of plywood. Make sure one edge of each piece of veneer extends past the jointed edges of the plywood, as shown in Figure 1. If you have more than eight pieces of veneer, make a second sandwich.

Pre-drill each sandwich for three sets of countersunk screws (see the Technical Drawings on page 39 for these locations). The pilot holes should be the full diameter of the screws in the top layer of plywood and in the veneers (to prevent splitting the delicate veneer), but only half the thickness of the screws in the lower piece of plywood, to provide some grab. Drive the screws, then use a bearing-guided flush trim bit to simultaneously create a straight edge along all the sheets of veneer in each sandwich, as shown at left.

Leaving the veneer in the sandwiches, set your table saw fence exactly 2¹⁄₁₆" from the blade. Rip the sandwiches into strips (see Figure 2), with the previously squared edges against the fence. If your veneer was a little over 4" wide, this process will yield two strips. If the veneer was wider, obviously you'll get more.

After ripping, pass both edges of each sandwich across the jointer, taking ¹⁄₃₂" on each pass. The screws will hold

the sandwich together, and the result will be sandwiches exactly 2" wide.

Crosscutting the Veneer into Squares

Here's the beauty of this production method: you can leave the veneers in their protective sandwiches all the way through the process until they are actually cut into perfect 2" squares. The next step is to attach a wide auxiliary fence to your table saw's miter

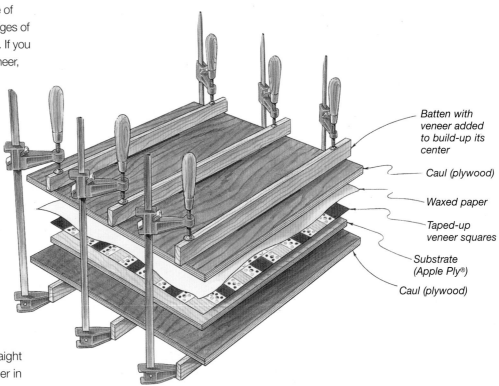

Batten with veneer added to build-up its center

Caul (plywood)

Waxed paper

Taped-up veneer squares

Substrate (Apple Ply®)

Caul (plywood)

Figure 4: *Use special, quick-sanding veneer tape to assemble the squares of veneer into a grid. Apply the tape to the best side.*

gauge, then place a stop on the fence exactly 2" past the far side of the blade (see Figure 3).

Install a fine crosscut blade with at least 60 teeth in the table saw. The sandwich and the auxiliary fence combine to provide zero clearance

support for the crosscuts, but a fine blade ensures there's no tearout. Trim the first end off a sandwich (including one set of the screws), then carefully proceed along the sandwich, making another cut every 2".

Taping the Squares Together

Once your all veneer squares are cut to size, lay them out on a tabletop and orient them so all the grain patterns run in the same direction. In the first row, you should have a white square on each player's right. Turn the best side up on each square, then start taping them together with veneer tape as shown in Figure 4. This is a special soft paper tape with holes in it to reduce the amount of coverage, and thus the amount of sanding required to remove

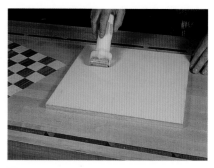

Figure 5: *Apply glue to the substrate only before stacking the assembly in your veneer press. Roll it out for even coverage.*

it. Make sure the lines are straight: a small gap won't hurt if it's necessary to keep everything aligned.

A Shop-built Veneer Press

To apply pressure to the center of the checkerboard as you glue it to the substrate, you'll need to build a veneer press (see the illustration on page 35) Inside of two sheets of scrap plywood (called cauls), you'll place the substrate, then the veneer, and on top of that a layer of wax paper.

The press applies pressure in the center first, and then to the outside edges. This is done by means of a series of battens—sticks that are thicker in the middle than at the ends. The easiest way to make them is to simply glue two layers of 7"-long veneer to the center of each piece of stock, as indicated in the illustration on page 35.

Apply standard yellow glue with a roller, spreading an even light coat on the substrate only (see Figure 5).

Carefully lay the taped-up veneer in place, briefly allow it to tack, then assemble the press and apply clamps to the battens.

Milling the V-grooves

After you remove the assembly from the press (give it a day to cure), sand it lightly

to remove any residual glue, but don't sand through the veneer.

Install a 45° V-groove bit in your router table and expose ¹⁄₁₆" of it above the tabletop. Make a pass on some scrap, adjusting the height if necessary. Plow the two center grooves in the board (see Figure 6), then move the fence 2" to make the next series of cuts. Plow four grooves this time, rotating the board 90° after each cut. Repeat the process to complete the decorative "V's." Use the same bit to chamfer the outside top edges of the board, then leave it in the router.

Completing the Molding

After you have ripped the molding to size, plow a groove into its top face using the same V-groove bit you did for the checkerboard's top (see the inset for Figure 6). The Technical Drawings on page 39 provide the exact location. Once that's completed, switch to a straight bit to mill the rabbet on the top of the molding (see Figure 7), and a matching rabbet on the bottom edges of the substrate. You can also use a dado blade to cut the substrate rabbet, as shown in Figure 7.

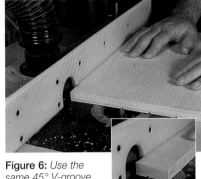

Figure 6: *Use the same 45° V-groove bit to plow the groove in the top of the frame (inset) as you did for the checkerboard grid.*

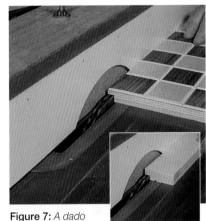

Figure 7: *A dado head in the table saw cuts rabbets in the substrate and the frame (inset).*

Figure 8: *Once you've completed the V-groove and rabbet on your molding, switch to a fine rip blade for the chamfer cut. Be sure to use a featherboard and push stick for this operation.*

---

*Quick*Tip

Project Support

With a roller, a knob with threaded ³⁄₈" stub, a ³⁄₈" insert, some screws and scrap hardwood, you can construct a roller stand to support long projects being drilled on your benchtop drill press. Outfit the base of the support with a square opening about ¹⁄₁₆" larger than the support piece on either side, so the support will easily slide into the base. To provide for varying heights, install a knob with a ¹⁄₈" threaded stub that presses a moveable block against the support. Install a threaded metal insert in the front block for the knob's stub.

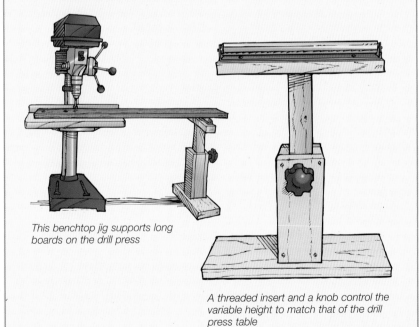

This benchtop jig supports long boards on the drill press

A threaded insert and a knob control the variable height to match that of the drill press table

Checkered History

Early in the last century, Sir Gardner Wilkinson discovered a portrayal of King Rameses playing checkers (or draughts) in the ancient temple of Thebes, circa 4000 B.C. This verified that the game had preceded chess. Checkers was introduced to Europe from Egypt around 1500 A.D.

Complete the molding by setting your table saw blade to 30° and chamfering the top outside edge (see Figure 8). Reset the blade to 90°, then sand the molding and miter it to length, dry-fitting it to the substrate as you do.

Glue-up and Finishing

If this were a picture you were framing, a coat of glue on the miters and a few clamps are all that would be needed to assemble the frame. However, a checkerboard gets a lot more use than a picture frame, so reinforce the miters with #0 biscuits. Cut the slots, apply the glue and clamp the frame together. Make sure it's both flat and square as you apply pressure with a band clamp (insert the board while clamping, as shown at left, but remove it before the glue sets).

After the glue has cured, apply a coat of glue to the rabbet in the frame and install the checkerboard. Secure it with spring clamps, using pads to protect the veneer. Clean up any glue squeeze-out immediately with a damp rag.

Sand the entire project with 220-grit paper, going easy on the veneer if you're using a power sander. Then apply three coats of clear satin polyurethane finish: it's durable enough to stand up to heavy use. Sand lightly between these coats with 320-grit paper, then hop in the car and go find some big sheets of gift wrapping paper! Chances are, you'll be way ahead of Santa for the next holiday season.

Door Exploded View

Shop Door Elevation

(Front View)

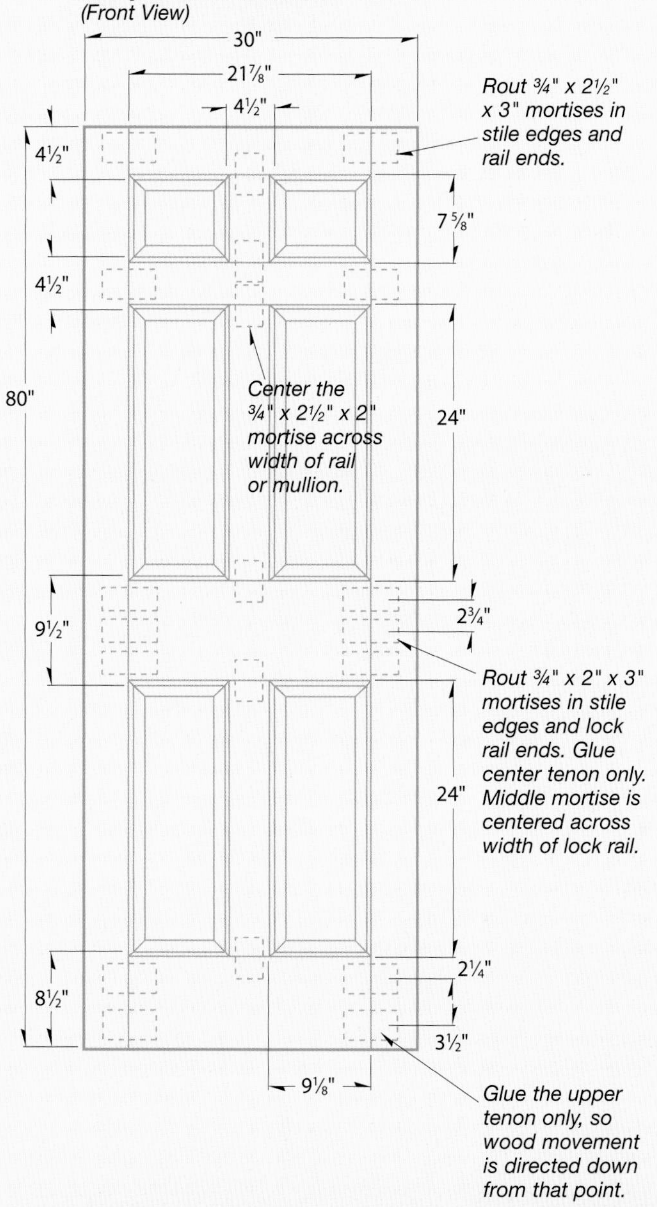

30"
21⅞"
4½"
4½"
7⅝"
4½"
80"
24"
9½"
2¾"
24"
8½"
2¼"
3½"
9⅛"
Rout ¾" x 2½" x 3" mortises in stile edges and rail ends.
Center the ¾" x 2½" x 2" mortise across width of rail or mullion.
Rout ¾" x 2" x 3" mortises in stile edges and lock rail ends. Glue center tenon only. Middle mortise is centered across width of lock rail.
Glue the upper tenon only, so wood movement is directed down from that point.

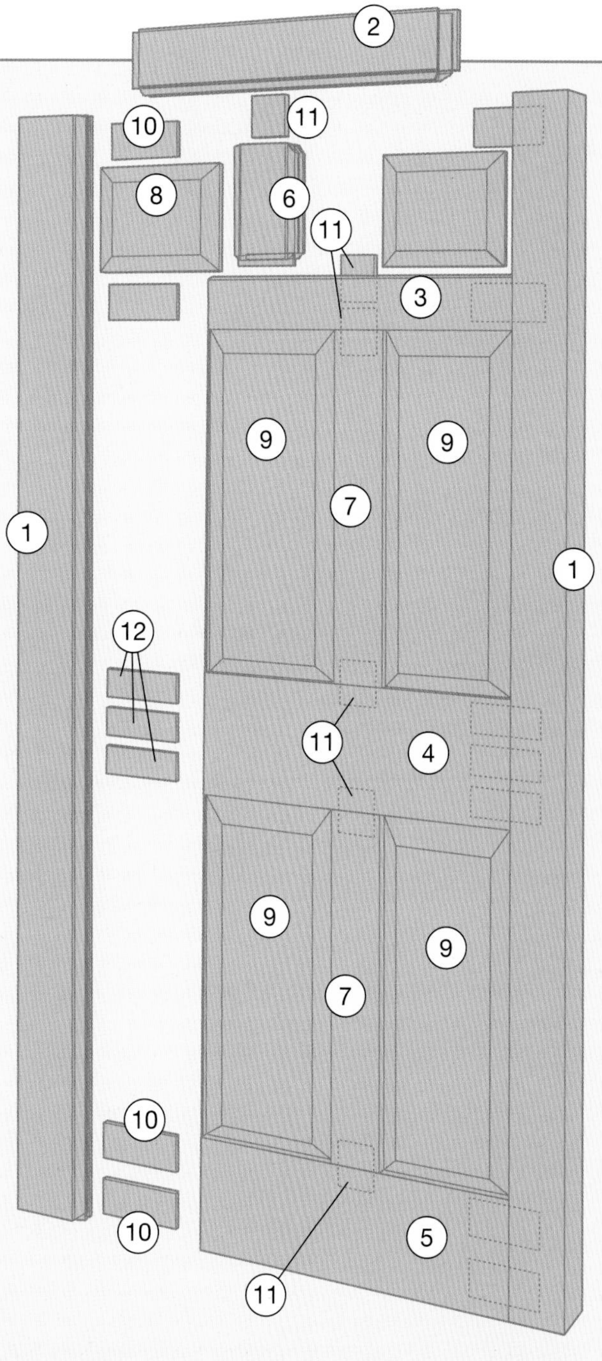

1
2
3
4
5
6
7
8
9
10
11
12

Material List – Shop Door

	T x W x L	
1 Stiles* (2)	1¾" x 4½" x 80"	6/4 poplar
2 Top Rail (1)	1¾" x 4½" x 21⅞"	6/4 poplar
3 Frieze Rail (1)	1¾" x 4½" x 21⅞"	6/4 poplar
4 Lock Rail (1)	1¾" x 9⅛" x 21⅞"	6/4 poplar
5 Bottom Rail (1)	1¾" x 8½" x 21⅞"	6/4 poplar
6 Frieze Mullion (1)	1¾" x 4½" x 7⅝"	6/4 poplar

	T x W x L	
7 Mullions (2)	1¾" x 4½" x 24"	6/4 poplar
8 Frieze Panels (2)	1¼" x 9⅛" x 7⅝"	
9 Middle/bottom Panels (4)	1¼" x 9⅛" x 24"	
10 Loose Tenons (8)	¾" x 2½" x 5⅞"	scraps
11 Loose Tenons (6)	¾" x 2½" x 4"	scraps
12 Loose Tenons (6)	¾" x 2" x 5⅞"	scraps

NOTE: *These dimensions are based on the use of Infinity bits. If you use Freud bits, rails and mullions must be slightly longer.*

**Work with pieces 4" to 6" longer than final length; trim excess after assembly. If you use Freud bits, the panels must be 1⅜" thick; start with 6/4 stock.*

By clamping the rails and mullions vertically in the mortising block (above), you can mill mortises in the ends accurately with a handheld plunge router (note the attached edge guide).

the part on the router mortising block fixture that I'll describe next. The mortising setup will control the position and size of the cut.

Label each joint with a letter or a number. The big value here comes

later, when you fit the individual tenons (which you can also label).

Now set up your mortising fixture. Years ago I designed and built a mortising block (see box on page 46) for routing mortises with a plunge router and edge guide. Plans for this shop-built fixture are in two of my books, *Bill Hylton's Power Tool Joinery* (F&W Publications) and the newly revised edition of *Woodworking with the Router* (Reader's Digest Books). Simple yet versatile and sturdy, it's basically a big block I clamp at the edge of the workbench. Here's how it works:

• The workpiece is clamped to the face of the block, so the edge or end to be mortised is flush with the block's top surface. It has interchangeable, adjustable workrests—one horizontal, one vertical—with toggle clamps to support and secure the workpiece.

• The plunge router rests on the top surface with the bit positioned over the workpiece. The top surface must be perpendicular to the face, of course. A registration line across the top is critical: It represents the center

The same mortising block also sets up the edge mortises in the stiles (above). You'll need to support the long free end with a workstand.

of the mortise, and you'll align the workpiece to it.

• The router's edge guide rides along the block's back edge (It's actually captured in a track.) The guide's setting controls the position of the

Two Pioneers of Passage- and Entry-door Router Bits

Infinity was first to market an architectural door set. Basically, they're pumped-up cope-and-stick bits designed to machine stock up to a full 1¾" thick in one pass. Until they appeared, routing architectural door parts required multiple passes with "doctored" cabinetry bits. What these specialty router bits do is no

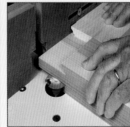

When you break down Freud's coping bit, the bottom profile cutter can mill an integral tenon of any length by shifting the fence.

less than what shaper cutters have done for decades. With Infinity's bit set, as with all shaper cutters intended for the same job, making strong joints is an entirely separate undertaking from milling the basic cope-and-stick connection.

Freud's new router-bit set, on the other hand, takes joint strength

Infinity's two bits are a bare pair. A ¼" slotter to use when working 1⅜"-thick stock is included, but there are no instructions for setting up or using the bits.

one step further. Its innovative cope cutter enables you to form an integral tenon as long as you want. After an initial cut that forms both copes and a stub tenon, you break down the bit by unscrewing an arbor holding a profile cutter and the pilot bearing. What you're left with is an inverted-head, pilot-free bit, still set for the cut. Additional passes, controlled by the

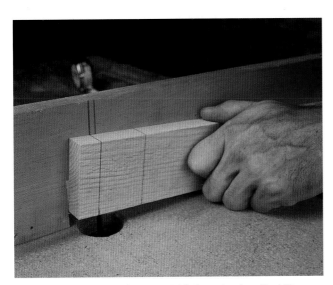

Figure 1: *Draw lines on the router table fence to show the bit's cutting area, then start and stop the mortise routing as your layout reaches the lines.*

You'll find patterns for the shelves, top rails, and front standards in the Technical Drawings on page 57. If you're planning to build more than one baker's shelf, make a hardboard template from these patterns for more consistent results.

Making Shelves and Standards

Begin working on your baker's shelf project by joining and gluing up a panel for the shelves (pieces 1). Make the panel at least 14" wide and 70" long so you can cut all four shelves from it. After the glue sets, scrape off the glue squeeze-out, then give the glue time to fully cure before planing the panel flat (planing too soon may result in a depression along each joint line as the water from the glue evaporates).

Next, plane a ¾" x 11" x 75" board flat and joint one edge perfectly straight. Rip the second edge parallel with the first and lay out the dadoes for the standards (pieces 2, 3, and 4), as shown in the Elevation Drawing on page 54. Install a ¾" dado blade in your table saw, raise the blade ¼" and screw a long auxiliary fence to your miter gauge to support the long board. Make a few test cuts in scrap wood to guarantee the accuracy of your miter gauge, then plow the four shelf dadoes.

Replace the dado blade with a ripping blade and cut the wide board into four narrow pieces for the standards,

following the dimensions in the Material List. Ripping the board with the dadoes facing up will reduce the amount of tearout at the dado walls.

Pass your jointer plane over the edges of each standard to make them square and flat, then reinstall the ¾" dado blade and rip a ¼"-deep rabbet along one edge of the rear left standard (piece 3). This rabbet aligns the two rear standards and increases the gluing area of the assembly for a stronger joint. Now you can see why the rear standards were ripped at different widths—when the right piece is fitted into the left, they appear to be the same size.

Lay out the holes for the dowels (pieces 5) and the mortises for the rails (pieces 6) on each standard, as shown in the Dowel and Dado Locations Drawing on page 54. Remember to group your standards into left and right subassemblies, or you may end up with pieces that can't fit together. Next, chuck a ⅜" brad point bit in your drill press and clamp a fence to the table to center your standard stock under the bit. Set the depth stop and bore the ¹³⁄₁₆"-deep dowel holes now.

To form the rail mortises in the standards, set up your router table with a ¼" straight bit and, once again, clamp a fence to the table to center the stock on the bit. Mark the fence to indicate the bit's cutting area, and use the marks for starting and stopping the cuts (see Figure 1). Be sure to rout the mortises in several shallow passes of increasing depth to ease the strain on the bit.

Trace the full-size pattern of the feet onto the front standards and cut them to shape with a jigsaw. Now file and sand these shaped edges before you begin the shelf assembly.

The holes in the standards could have been drilled with a ½" bit for joining the ½"-diameter dowels (pieces 5). This would make the project easier, but it would diminish the strength of the assembly. Instead, ⅜"-diameter holes leave more "meat" around the joints, to reduce the chance of splitting, and the tenon shoulders greatly improve the rigidity of the overall structure.

Cutting Tenons on Dowels

Cut the dowels to length using a jig like the one shown in Figure 2—a few extra will come in handy. Next, chuck a ½" straight bit in your router table and clamp a fence to the table so it just grazes the bit. Normally, using a fence with an

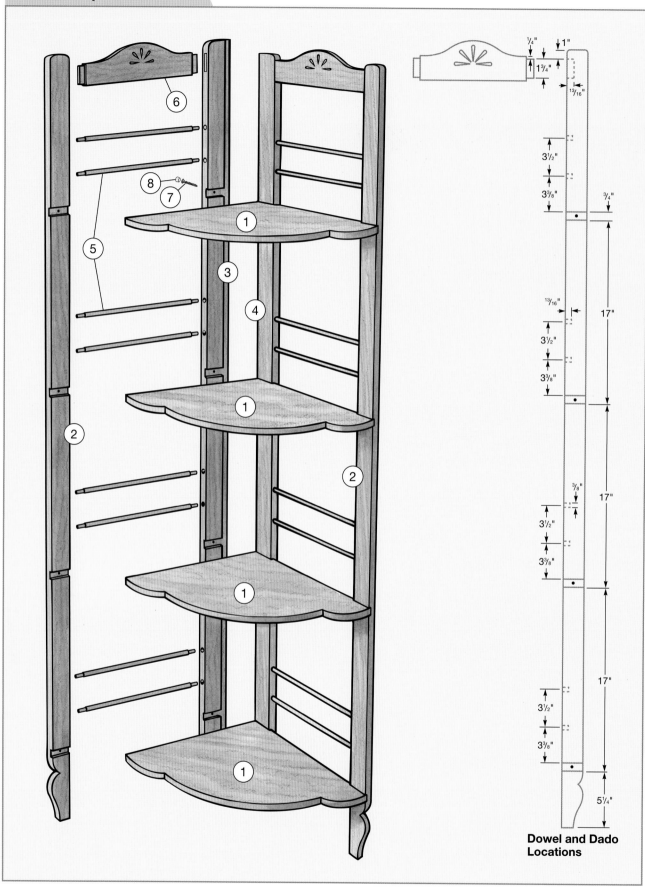

Dowel and Dado Locations

Figure 2: *To improve the safety of cutting dowels to length, construct a simple table saw sled that rides in the miter gauge slots with a V-groove to support the dowel.*

Figure 3: *Clamp a stop block to the router table fence and slowly rotate your dowels over the ½" straight bit to form the ⅜" x ¾" round tenons.*

exhaust hole would be best, but in this case a fence without a hole will provide better support and minimize vibration while routing the dowel tenons. Clamp a stop block to the table so you can cut ¾"-long tenons (see Figure 3). Now raise the bit ¹⁄₁₆" and slide a dowel over the bit, turning it slowly to cut a sample tenon. Check the fit of the tenon in a standard hole, make any adjustments, and cut another sample tenon. Once you have a perfect fit, meaning that the tenon slips into the hole with only slight resistance, rout tenons on both ends of all the dowels.

To make inserting the dowel tenons into the holes a little easier, and to provide some glue relief, chamfer the end of each tenon. Clamp a belt sander upside down to your workbench and spin the end of each tenon against the running belt. Leaving the tenon ends square could cause excessive hydraulic pressure in the holes as the dowels are installed, possibly causing the standards to split or the tenons to stop shy of seating in their holes.

Material List

		T x W x L
1	Shelves (4)	¾" x 13" x 20½"
2	Front Standards (2)	¾" x 2" x 72"
3	Rear Lt. Standard (1)	¾" x 2¾" x 72"
4	Rear Rt. Standard (1)	¾" x 2¼" x 72"
5	Dowels (16)	½" x 11⅝"
6	Rails (2)	¾" x 4" x 11⅝"
7	Screws (16)	#8-1¼"
8	Plugs (16)	⅜" Diameter

Making the Top Rails

Cut stock for the rails (pieces 6), making sure the edges are ripped parallel to each other, and double check to see that the ends are perfectly square. Before bandsawing the top edge of each piece, form tenons on the rail ends where they will join the standard mortises. Install a ½" dado blade in your table saw and clamp a set-up block to the fence. Adjust the fence to cut ¾"-long tenons and raise the blade ¼". Cut a sample tenon on some scrap wood and test the fit in a mortise. When you're satisfied with the fit, cut the tenon cheeks on the rail stock, then turn the pieces on edge and cut the bottom shoulders using the exact same set-up.

It's best to rout the sunburst on each rail now, while there's still plenty of stock to support your router. Cut out the full-size pattern of the rail and trace the sunburst and top edge outlines onto each piece. Next, chuck a V-groove bit in your router and adjust the depth stop to permit a ³⁄₁₆"-deep cut. Using your router freehand, rout away the waste within each ray of the sunburst, staying about ¹⁄₁₆" inside the lines. Next, use a V-tool, a veining tool and a ⅜" chisel to complete the carvings (see Figure 4).

Bandsaw the rails to shape and sand the curved edges smooth. Cut ¼"-deep shoulders on the top edge of each tenon with a fine-toothed handsaw and a chisel, then use a file to round over the edges of the tenons until they fit into the routed mortises. Try assembling each set of standards with the dowels and rail, without using glue, to make sure all the parts fit properly.

Pulling the Skeleton Together

Now that all the standard components are made, you can assemble the structure of the baker's shelf. It's best to assemble the project in stages, first constructing one pair

Figure 4: *After removing most of the waste with a router and V-groove bit, complete the sunburst carvings with a little handwork using a V tool, a veining tool and a chisel.*

Figure 5: *The rabbet automatically registers the rear standard assembly, but make sure the dadoes line up before tightening the clamps completely.*

of standards with their dowels and rail, and then the other set. Don't bother with the shelves until after the two sets of standards have been joined.

Organize your pieces into the two subassembly groups, then spread glue in all the dowel holes and mortises of one set. Install the dowels and rail in one standard and draw the second standard into place with clamps. Repeat this procedure on the second set, and shave off any glue squeeze-out with a chisel once it becomes rubbery. Remove the subassemblies after clamping them for a few hours and center a counterbored pilot hole at each dado location (see the Dowel and Dado Locations Drawing).

Sand the rail joints flush on each subassembly and shape the top ends of the standards with a jigsaw and file, following the pattern shown in the Technical Drawings on page 57. Spread glue in the rabbet of the left subassembly and clamp the two subassemblies together (see Figure 5). Allow the glue to dry, checking to see that the angle between the two sides remains at exactly 90°. After the glue dries you may need to blend the shaping at the top of the rear standards.

Cutting the Shelves

By now you can plane the shelf panel and rip it to width. Once again, make sure the panel edges are parallel. Next, cut out a full-size pattern of the shelf and make a hardboard template. Trace the shelf profile onto the panel, alternating

the direction as you go to fit in all four shelves. Leave at least ½" between each layout to allow room for cutting out the shapes. Separate the shelves by cutting between the layout lines with a jigsaw.

Once the four shelves are roughly separated they're easier to handle on the table saw. Turn your miter gauge to its 45° setting and make some sample cuts to see how accurate the set-up is. The corner created by the two cuts on your sample should be dead square so the shelves fit properly in the standards. Fine-tune the miter gauge to achieve a perfect test cut, then trim the edges of each shelf to the layout lines.

Sand the shelf surfaces, then slip the shelves into the dadoes in the standards. Extend the pilot holes from the standards into the shelves, and mark each shelf where it passes out of the front standards, as shown in the drawing below. Align the template with each set of marks and trace the front edge pattern onto the shelves. Cut the shelves to shape with a jigsaw outfitted with a fine-toothed blade, as shown in Figure 6, then use a file to refine the curves, if necessary. Sand the edges of the shelves with a palm sander. Avoid rounding over the side edges to maintain crisp corners in the dado joints.

Spread glue into the dadoes in the standards and slip the shelves into place. Drive a screw (pieces 7) into each pilot hole and cover the screw heads by gluing plugs (pieces 8) into all the counterbores. Trim the plugs flush.

Finishing Up

Sand the project through the grits up to 180 and wipe it with mineral spirits to expose any hidden dried glue spots or sanding scratches. Ease all the sharp edges and blend the joint areas into smooth transitions. You can stain your baker's shelf as we did here or leave it natural, then apply a coat of sanding sealer and two coats of varnish. Be sure to sand lightly between topcoats with 400-grit wet/dry paper.

Whether you need a rack for cooling your and pies, or just want to show off your favorite country collectibles, setting aside a weekend to build this baker's shelf will be time well spent. Best of all, it'll be a great weekend of building time in the shop.

Figure 6: *After laying out the shelf profiles so they intersect the front edge of the standards, cut the shelves to shape with a jigsaw.*

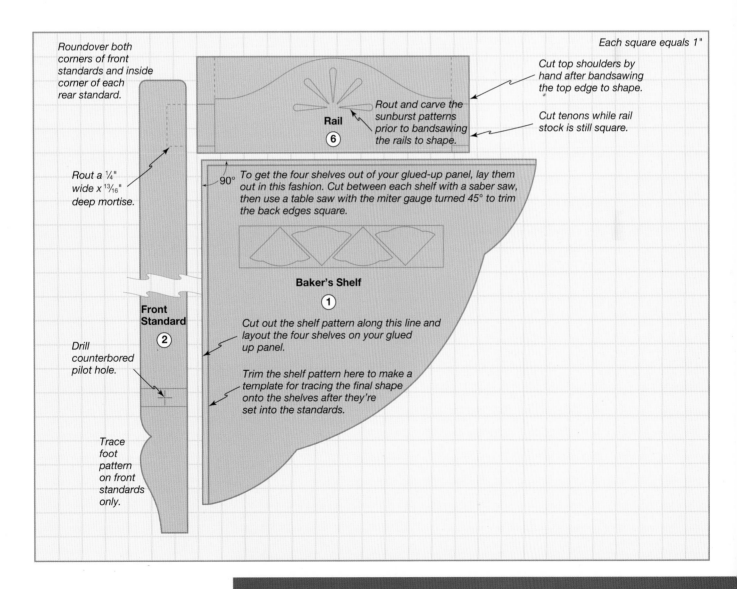

Each square equals 1"

Roundover both corners of front standards and inside corner of each rear standard.

Cut top shoulders by hand after bandsawing the top edge to shape.

Rout and carve the sunburst patterns prior to bandsawing the rails to shape.

Rail
6

Cut tenons while rail stock is still square.

Rout a ¹⁄₄" wide x ¹³⁄₁₆" deep mortise.

90°

To get the four shelves out of your glued-up panel, lay them out in this fashion. Cut between each shelf with a saber saw, then use a table saw with the miter gauge turned 45° to trim the back edges square.

Baker's Shelf
1

Front Standard
2

Cut out the shelf pattern along this line and layout the four shelves on your glued up panel.

Drill counterbored pilot hole.

Trim the shelf pattern here to make a template for tracing the final shape onto the shelves after they're set into the standards.

Trace foot pattern on front standards only.

To cut his top to shape, the author uses a hewing hatchet, which is sharpened with a single bevel on one side. The tool does a surprisingly quick and effective job of shaping wood, especially when preceded by scoring cuts to relieve pressure.

Demi-Lune Sofa Table

In some ways, this demi-lune table is an imposter. Despite its curves, it's easier to make than it looks, whether you use hand tools as we show here or or power tools. From first glance, the table also appears to be made of mahogany and crotch birch, but it's actually a faux painted finish over ordinary softwood. What's true through and through is that the half-moon shape makes it an ideal choice for a hall or sofa table.

by Stephen Shepherd

A demi-lune table is a classical furniture form that takes its name from the half-moon shape of its top. This top may be either semi-circular or elliptical. The continuous curve on the front of the table makes it a good choice for narrow spaces, while its straight back edge is ideally suited for placement where it will not be seen.

Typically a demi-lune table typically has two legs at the back corners and two legs spaced roughly equally across the curved front. Traditionally, these legs have been turned or square-tapered. The legs are connected by four apron rails, including a straight rail at the back and three curved rails across the front. For aesthetic reasons, many woodworkers prefer to make the front center rail longer than the other two curved rails.

Some demi-lune tables are extravagantly made, with expensive hardwoods, parquetry and inlays. This one is more provincial. It is painted and grained to imitate mahogany (see detail photo, page 62). We also painted gold stripes on the upper parts of the tapered legs. Because this table essentially has a painted finish, we were able to employ inexpensive, widely available materials: standard ¾"-thick lumberyard pine for the top and the back rail and 2"-thick spruce for the legs and front apron.

Overall, the table shown here is 30" tall by 30" wide by only 11¼" deep, but feel free to vary the dimensions to suit your purpose. Our author made his table entirely by hand with simple hand tools, but you can just as easily use power tools for this project to shortcut some of the steps.

The completed table features details that lead a casual observer to imagine gold inlay and fine veneers.

Legs
(Side Views)

3/4"   3/4"

3"   4"   3"

1/4"   1/4"

1/2"   1/2"

5   5

29 1/4"

25 1/4"

1"   1"
1 1/2"   1 1/2"

1/4"
1/4"   (Bottom   1 1/2"
Views)
1/2"   1/2"

Front
Leg

Rear
Leg

NOTE: The
table's front
legs are
tapered on
three sides
while the rear
legs are only
tapered on
the inside
and front
aspect
(see Bottom
Views).

The curved aprons
are cut from a thick
piece of wood,
so the grain on
their tenons will be
"short." Take care as
you bring the aprons
and legs together that you
don't break off the tenons.

NOTE: While this table is constructed
from inexpensive softwood stock
(available at most local home centers),
it is painted to mimic more expensive
hardwood. The goal is not to create a
photographic recreation of hardwood,
but to simply give the impression and
let the viewer's mind "fill in the blanks."

Material List – Table

		T x W x L
1 Tabletop (1)		3/4" x 11 1/4" x 30"
2 Front Apron (1)		2" x 4" x 12 1/4"
3 Side Aprons (2)		2" x 4" x 10 1/4"
4 Back Apron (1)		3/4" x 4" x 25 1/2"
5 Legs (4)		1 1/2" x 1 1/2" x 29 1/4"

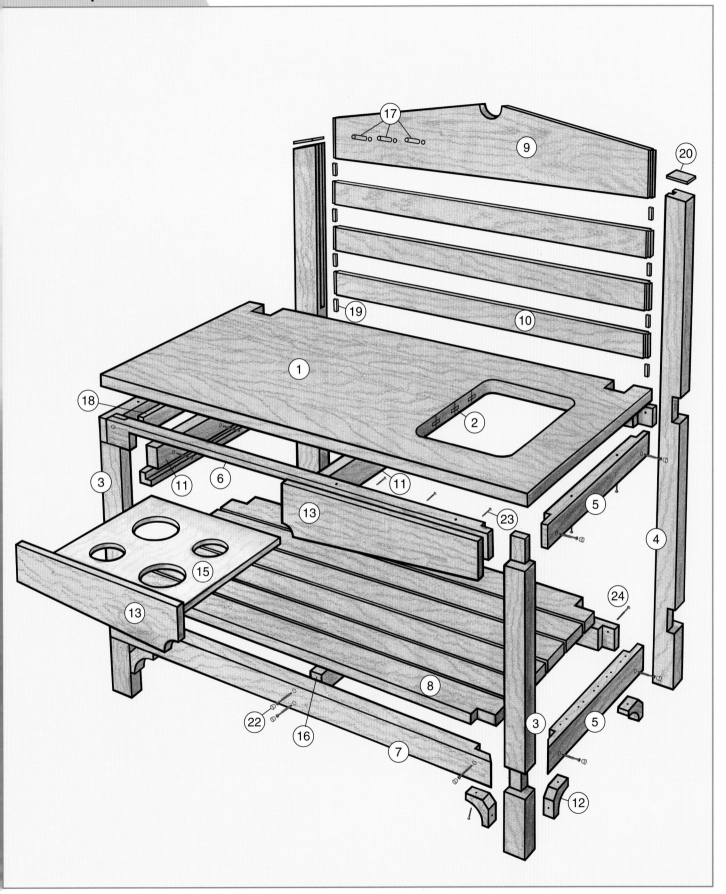

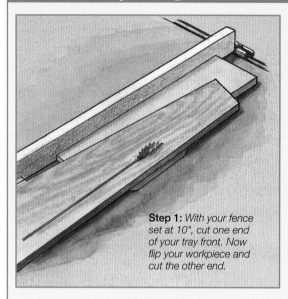

Step 1: *With your fence set at 10", cut one end of your tray front. Now flip your workpiece and cut the other end.*

Cutting the tapers on the tray front and the top back board of the potting bench is easy with this simple jig, even though the tray front is 4" longer than the top back board. Cut the jig and spacer from ¾" birch plywood, as shown in the illustration at left, using your table saw and jigsaw.

Now just follow the two-step process shown below.

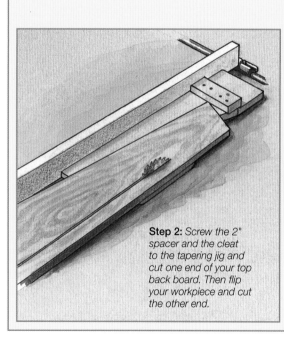

Step 2: *Screw the 2" spacer and the cleat to the tapering jig and cut one end of your top back board. Then flip your workpiece and cut the other end.*

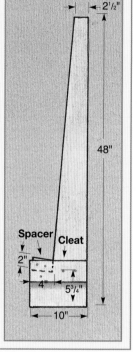

Finish up on the drill press by cutting holes for the tool hangers (pieces 17) at a 5° angle tipped upward on the top back board. This angle ensure that tools won't fall off the dowel pegs later.

Putting the Pieces Together

Now it's time to put the pieces together. With the help of some clamps, dry-assemble the legs and aprons, making sure everything fits precisely and the full assembly is square. Once you're satisfied, drill ⅛" pilot holes and ⅜" counterbores where they are marked on the Technical Drawings on pages 80 and 81.

Now unclamp the dry assembly and call a buddy who can supply a couple of extra hands. Brush on water-resistant glue, then re-clamp and screw the pieces together. We used square-drive exterior screws for making these connections. Square-drive screws are finally becoming readily available at most lumber yards and hardware stores. Once you use them, you'll be sorely tempted to throw away every slotted or phillips screw you own. You'll need a square drive bit for installing these screws. Some manufacturers include a bit with the screws if you buy them in volume. We've found that square drive screws are worth every penny, simply because the design seldom if ever slips.

Once this assembly dries, glue and screw the tray spacer (piece 18) in place and attach the tray runners (see Technical Drawings on pages 80 and 81).

Now tip the bench on its back to tackle the top and shelf. Clamp the top in place and use an awl to mark the locations of the screw holes (see Figure 5). Remove the top and drill the ⅛" pilot holes 1" deep, then replace the top and screw it in place. Follow the same procedure with the shelf boards, but first sand a roundover on the top edges.

Mark the screw hole locations on the aprons and the shelf stretcher (piece 16) as indicated on the Technical Drawings on pages 80 and 81. With a 9⁄64" bit in your drill press and a fence set ⅞" from center, drill all the way through the aprons. Now switch to a ⅜" countersink and set your depth stop to form a 1"-deep counterbore. Drill the holes on one edge of an apron and flip your workpiece to drill the matching holes, using the 9⁄64" pilot hole as a guide. Follow the same procedures on the rest of the aprons and the stretcher.

Figure 5: *With the top firmly clamped to the aprons, tip the bench on its back and mark the locations of the pilot holes with an awl.*

Attach the two notched shelf boards first, and follow with the other four boards spaced an equal distance apart. As long as you have the bench on its back, now is a good time to glue and screw the corner brackets in place beneath the lower aprons.

Return the bench to an upright position and glue the spacers (pieces 19) and back boards—but not the top back board—in place. Dry-fit the top board just to make sure the taper you've marked on the board meets the top of the taper you've already cut on the rear legs.

Tapering the Top Back Board and Tray Front

The tapering jig that's described in the sidebar on the preceding page is different than most jigs because it will cut the same taper on boards of different lengths. With this project, we wanted the arcs and tapers to match, even though the top back board is four inches shorter than the tray front.

Cut the taper on the top back board and glue it in place. The tool hangers are glued in place along with the leg caps (pieces 20), which protect the end grain of the rear legs and cover the grooves cut for the back board tenons.

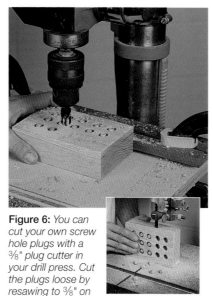

Figure 6: *You can cut your own screw hole plugs with a ⅜" plug cutter in your drill press. Cut the plugs loose by resawing to ⅜" on your band saw.*

Cut the tray front in half. Screw—but don't glue—the left half to the potting tray, using the tray cleat (piece 21) and 1¼" exterior-grade screws. Don't glue the plywood tray in place so you can easily replace it when necessary after a few seasons of use. Slide this half into the tray runners and

then glue and screw the right half to the front apron, making sure that it lines up with the left half.

Finishing Up

Cut ⅜"-diameter screw hole plugs (pieces 22) from white oak using a tapered plug cutter (see Figure 6). Glue the plugs in the screw holes on the front and side surfaces and use a sharp chisel to pare them evenly with the surrounding surface.

Sand the project with 80-, 120-, and 180-grit papers before applying two coats of satin spar marine varnish, sanding lightly with 180-grit paper between coats to ensure good adhesion. Your potting bench is now ready for many seasons of good use. Renew the topcoat with another layer of varnish every few years.

*Quick*Tip

Nailing a Sticky Situation

Unless you use your glue regularly, you've probably experienced the hassle of "skimmed-over" bottles of glue from time to time. Here's one trick for extending your glue's life: simply insert a tight-fitting nail in the spout and slowly turn it upside down, sealing the air out of the area of the spout inside the bottle. If the bottle still has a good spout, squeeze out as much air as possible and skip the nail. Then store the bottle upside-down in a coffee can. This way, any glue "skin" that may still form will end up on the bottom of the bottle when your turn the glue upright again, which won't clog the nozzle. Also, be sure to store your glue in a warm environment at all times to keep it from freezing; if you have a garage shop, bring your glue indoors during the winter months.

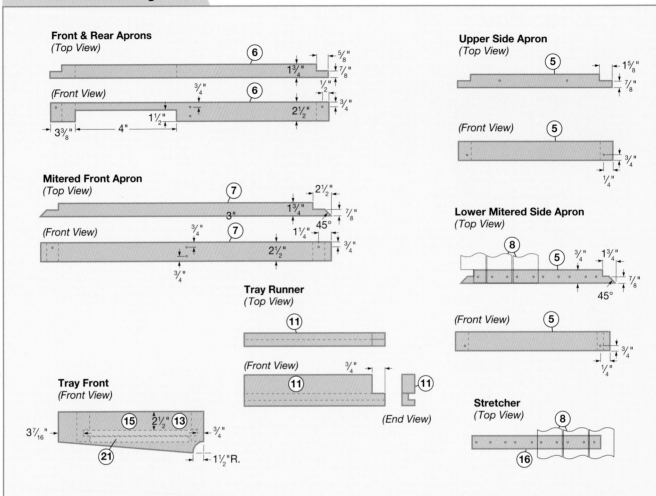

Front & Rear Aprons
(Top View)

(Front View)

Mitered Front Apron
(Top View)

(Front View)

Tray Runner
(Top View)

(Front View)

(End View)

Tray Front
(Front View)

Upper Side Apron
(Top View)

(Front View)

Lower Mitered Side Apron
(Top View)

(Front View)

Stretcher
(Top View)

Material List

	T x W x L		T x W x L
1 Bench Top (1)	1½" x 22¾" x 44"	**13** Tray Front (1)	¾" x 5½" x 40"
2 Bench Top Splines (5)	¼" x ¾" x 38"	**14** Mixing Tub (1)	Plastic Dishpan
3 Front Legs (2)	1¾" x 2½" x 34½"	**15** Potting Tray (1)	¾" x 15¾" x 19⅝"
4 Rear Legs (2)	1¾" x 2½" x 50¼"	**16** Shelf Stretcher (1)	1¾" x 2½" x 17½"
5 Side Aprons (4)	1¾" x 2½" x 21"	**17** Tool Hangers (3)	¼" x 2" Dowel
6 Front & Rear Aprons (3)	1¾" x 2½" x 38¼"	**18** Tray Spacer (1)	¾" x 2⅛" x 17½"
7 Mitered Front Apron (1)	1¾" x 2½" x 40"	**19** Back Board Spacers (8)	½" x ½" x 1"
8 Shelf Boards (6)	1½" x 3³⁄₁₆" x 40"	**20** Leg Caps (2	¼" x 1¾" x 2½"
9 Top Back Board (1)	¾" x 5½" x 36"	**21** Potting Tray Cleat (1)	¾" x ¾" x 13½"
10 Lower Back Boards (3)	¾" x 2" x 36"	**22** Screw Hole Plugs (15)	⅜" Dia. White Oak
11 Tray Runners (2)	1¾" x 4⅛" x 19¼"	**23** Exterior-grade Screws (10)	#6 x 1¼"
12 Corner Brackets (6)	1¾" x 3¼" x 3¼"	**24** Exterior-grade Screws (73)	#8 x 2½"

Figure 4:
The vertical grain on the ends of the drawer supports is a T-molding ripped from the edge of a board and glued into a dado.

to these supports. Cut the washers to size and countersink the screw heads. Then apply finish to both supports, because after installation, they're impossible to reach.

Wrapping Up the Bureau Carcass

The fall front supports are held in place by a frame that surrounds the large pencil drawer. This frame is composed of a top rail (piece 14) and two short stiles (pieces 15). Cut the parts to size, dry-fit them in the opening and adjust as necessary. Screw and glue them together and position the two fall front supports in place, then screw and glue the drawer frame in the opening, as shown in Figure 5, below.

The bureau top (piece 16) is supported by the sides and also by a cleat (piece 17) attached to the plywood back. Cut this cleat to size and install it flush with the top of the plywood, using predrilled and countersunk screws and glue.

Glue up the panel for the top, trim it to size, and profile the side and front edges (refer to Figure 6 on page 104). Shape it with a bearing-guided beading bit in your hand-held router.

Two moldings need to be attached to the underside of the bureau top before the top can be installed on the carcass. These pieces of straight stock—a door stop (piece 18) and a top rail (piece 19)—both get a 20° bevel ripped along one edge. After cutting them to size and creating their bevels, dry-fit all parts to check their fit and to mark their locations. Sand both pieces and attach the rail to the top and the stop to the rail, using glue and screws (predrill and countersink the holes).

With that done, you can secure the top to the bureau using a dozen 2" screws (predrill and countersink the holes), driving them down through the top.

Building the Bookcase Carcass

It's a good idea to complete the bookcase carcass next. That will allow you to build all the doors at the same time. The blanks for the sides of the bookcase (pieces 2) were glued up earlier, so the next step here is to match them to the bureau sides for a continuous grain pattern. After trimming them to size, lay out and mill two sliding dovetails in each side (see Figure 7 on page 105, inset), noting that the top dado is farther from the end of each board than the bottom one. Glue up panels for the bookcase top and bottom (pieces 20 and 21) and trim them to size. Sand the panels, then mill a sliding dovetail on both ends of each panel (see Figure 7). As always, be sure to test the set-up on scrap first before committing the parts.

Use a bearing-guided rabbeting bit to mill the rabbet on the back edge of each of the bookcase sides, top and bottom. Then assemble the bookcase with glue and clamps, making sure it is square and flat as you go.

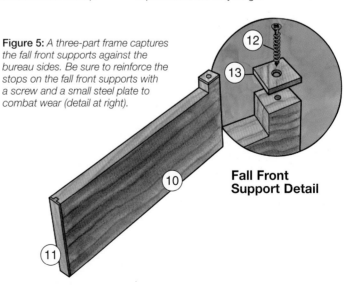

Figure 5: *A three-part frame captures the fall front supports against the bureau sides. Be sure to reinforce the stops on the fall front supports with a screw and a small steel plate to combat wear (detail at right).*

Fall Front Support Detail

After the assembly dries, glue and clamp three thin strips (pieces 22) to the bottom of the bookcase (see Figure 8 on page 105) to keep things stable when you place it on the bureau.

Note that the back of the bookcase is a series of narrow boards (pieces 23, 24, and 25) that are given a tongue and groove treatment. The two outside boards are different widths than those in the field, to accommodate hidden tongues and grooves. After dry fitting, use a chamfering bit to ease the edges where the boards will meet inside the bookcase (see Figure 9).

Install the back boards with screws driven through pre-bored, countersunk holes into the wide rabbets you milled earlier in the back edges of the bookcase components. Don't use glue: they have to be free to move.

Making the Bureau Drawer

This is a heavy-duty drawer designed with dovetail joinery to last a century or more. Cut the sides, front and back (pieces 26 and 27) to size, then use a commercial dovetailing jig to create the half-blind joinery in the corners, as shown in the illustrations on page 105. Plow stopped grooves in the drawer front and back, and through grooves into the sides, to accommodate the drawer bottom (piece 28). Assemble the drawer with glue and clamps, but don't glue the bottom in its grooves, to allow for movement.

Building the Bureau Doors

Two arch-top doors dress out the bureau and hide whatever you choose to store in the bureau. The components include two arched top

QuickTip

Glue-tight Joints

The easiest way to keep wet glue from leaking out of a fresh joint is to use a sharp utility knife or a rotary cutter in a multi-tool to score a small V-shaped channel just out of sight on the hidden parts of the joint. The groove should be about ⅛" in from the edge. Glue traveling toward the edge should pool in this groove and stay out of sight.

rails, a pair of straight bottom rails, four stiles and two glued-up panels (pieces 29 through 32).

After cutting all the parts to size, lay out the arches on the top rails (see the Elevation Drawings on page 108). Band saw the rails to shape, then tape them together to drum-sand the curves. Use a bearing-guided rabbeting bit in your router table to plow grooves in all of the door stiles and rails for the panels, as shown in Figure 10.

Glue up stock for the two door panels and plane it to thickness. Now dry-clamp the components together and use them as templates to lay out the shapes of the panels on your blank (see Figure 11). Extend the dimension of the panels by adding ⅜" to the marked-out shape on the top, bottom and side (so they'll be captured by the stile and rail grooves). Next, band-saw the panels to their final shape.

Figure 6:
The edge of the bureau top is profiled on its top and bottom with a bearing-guided beading bit.

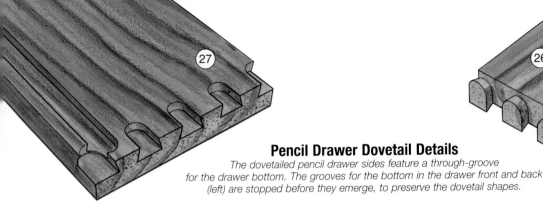

Pencil Drawer Dovetail Details

The dovetailed pencil drawer sides feature a through-groove for the drawer bottom. The grooves for the bottom in the drawer front and back (left) are stopped before they emerge, to preserve the dovetail shapes.

Figure 7: *The bookcase carcass is assembled with sliding dovetail joints milled with a ½", 14° bit in a router table.*

Figure 8: *Three spacers under the bookcase provide a solid, stable footing when it sits on top of the bureau and gets screwed in place.*

Figure 9: *After fashioning tongues and grooves on the boards for the bookcase back, gently chamfer the visible (inside) edges.*

Glue and clamp the doors together, making sure that the panels are not glued into their grooves. After the glue cures, dry-fit them in the opening and make any minor adjustments required to perfect the fit.

Constructing the Fall Front

The fall front is made up of two stiles, two rails and a panel (pieces 33 through 35). After cutting these pieces

Figure 10: *Plow the grooves for the panels in the curved door rails using a bearing-guided rabbeting bit.*

to size, plow a groove centered on the inside edge of each of the four frame components, using a bearing-guided rabbeting bit (see the Elevation Drawings on page 109). Adjust the bit height to create tongues on the ends of the stiles, then dry-fit the frame.

The panel becomes the writing surface, so it is built to fit the frame as tightly as possible. This means there is very little room for movement: it needs to be cut from a kiln-dried, quartersawn board with tight growth rings.

Mill the panel to size and use your bearing-guided rabbeting bit to form a rabbet on all four edges. Test the fit and make adjustments before gluing and clamping the fall front together. Check for square as you apply clamping pressure, and only apply glue on the stile/rail joints.

Adding the Bookcase Crown

The first element in the bookcase's built-up crown molding is a backer (piece 36) that is glued and screwed

in place. Drive the screws up through the bookcase top into pre-drilled, countersunk holes.

A large chamfered molding (piece 37) caps the built-up crown. Rip one edge to 35° on the table saw, rip the molding to width, then miter it to fit and attach it with glue and screws. The screws are driven from the inside into pre-drilled, countersunk holes.

Figure 11: *Dry-clamp the doors together and use them as templates to mark the shape of the panel. Add 5⁄16" all round for the groove.*

Bookcase Exploded View

Bookcase Side
(Inside View)

(37) 35°

(39)

(40)

2³⁄₈"
4¹⁄₄"

(2)

³⁄₄"

1¹⁄₈"

(22)

Bookcase Molding and Rail Assembly
(Side View)

(37)

(39)

(46)

(40)

(38)

(2)

Back Slat Chamfer Detail

³⁄₈"
¹⁄₄"

Chamfer

Material List – Bookcase

		T x W x L
20	Bookcase Top (1)	¾" x 10" x 33⁵⁄₈"
21	Bookcase Bottom (1)	¾" x 10" x 33⁵⁄₈"
22	Spacers (3)	¾" x ½" x 33"
23	Left Bookcase Back Slat (1)	¾" x 4¹¹⁄₁₆" x 37⁷⁄₈"
24	Right Bookcase Back Slat (1)	¾" x 4⁵⁄₁₆" x 37⁷⁄₈"
25	Field Bookcase Back Slats (7)	¾" x 4" x 37⁷⁄₈"

Bookcase Back Assembly
(Top View)

(23) (25) (24)

4⁵⁄₁₆"   3⁵⁄₈"   4⁵⁄₁₆"

Figure 12: *Secure the bookcase top rail to the carcass with glue, clamps, and a couple of screws, which will eventually be covered.*

Attach the bookcase top rail (piece 38) next. Two screws secure it to the sides, while glue and clamps attach it to the underside of the bookcase (see Figure 12). These screws will eventually be covered.

The second chamfered molding (piece 39) is ripped to size and shaped with a bearing-guided chamfering bit. Miter it to length and glue and clamp it in place.

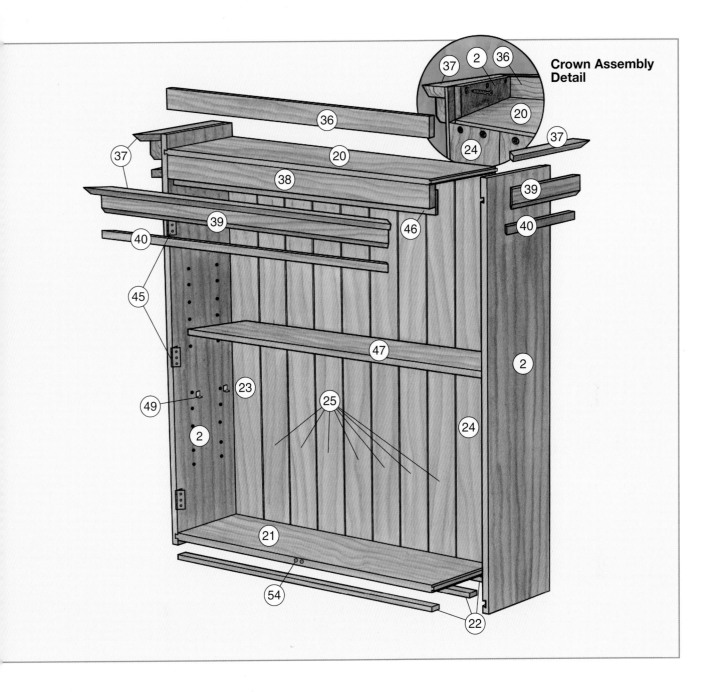

Crown Assembly Detail

A third molding (piece 40) completes the crown. It's a square piece of stock that is mitered and glued in place at the top of the door opening and the sides of the case.

Adding the Bookcase Doors

Building the glass inset doors is the most complex phase of construction in this project. Begin by cutting all parts to the dimensions shown in the Material List on pages 154 and 155. The first operation is the creation of tenons on the ends of all four rails (pieces 41). The cheek on one side of each tenon is ⅜" deeper than that on the other, as shown in Figure 13. Trim the shoulders flush with the shorter cheek using a dado head in the table saw (see Figure 14).

A bearing-guided rabbeting bit chucked in a table-mounted router makes the rabbet on the inside edge of each rail and stile (pieces 42). Then it's time to fire up the mortising machine to chop the two mortises in each stile.

If you dry-fit the tenons to the mortises, you'll see that there's a small amount of material on either side of each mortise that still has to be removed. A rabbeting bit set for a ½" cut takes care of the material at the end of the workpiece. You can chop the

Drawer & Door Exploded Views

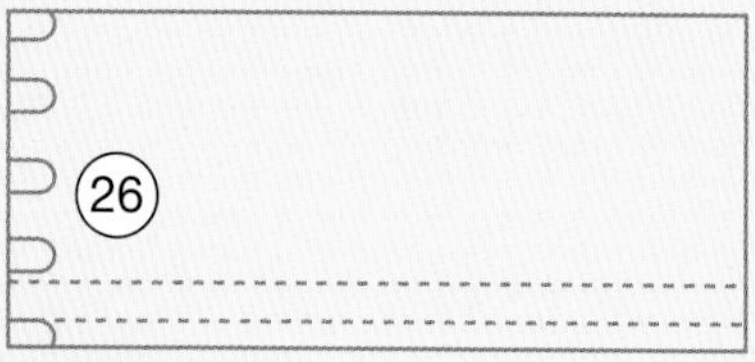

Dovetail Layout

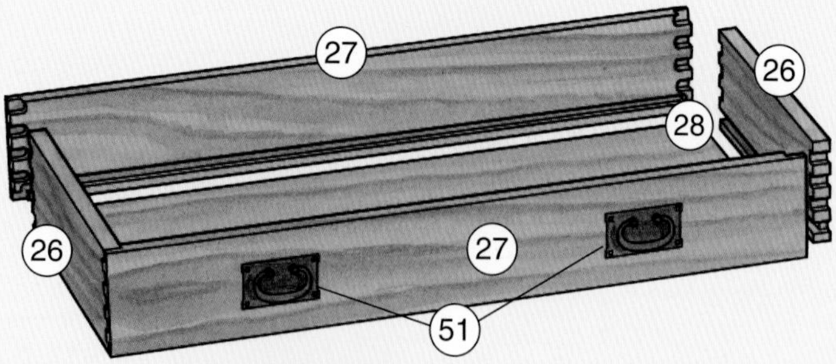

Pencil Drawer Exploded View

Bureau Door Exploded View

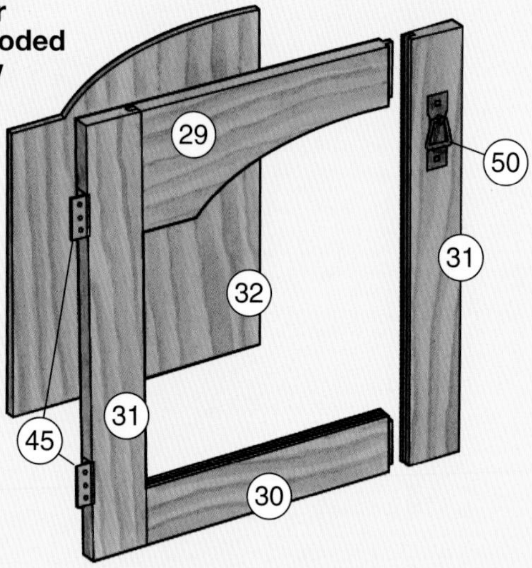

Bureau Door
(Top and Front Views)

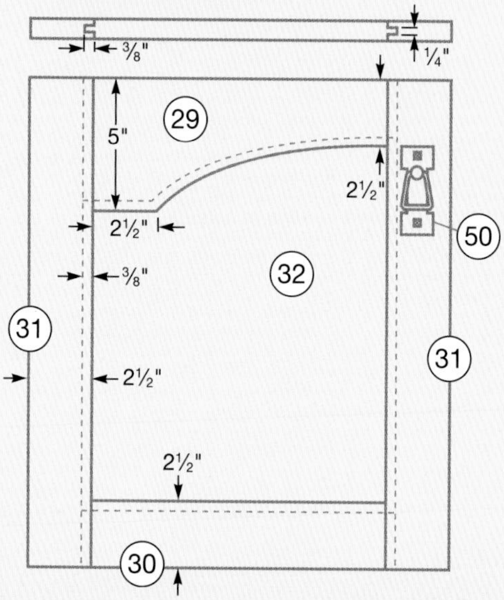

Material List – Drawers & Fall Front

	T x W x L
26 Pencil Drawer Sides (2)	¾" x 4⅜" x 12½"
27 Pencil Drawer Front & Back (2)	¾" x 4⅜" x 29⅞"
28 Pencil Drawer Bottom (1)	½" x 12½" x 28⅞"
29 Top Bureau Door Rails (2)	¾" x 5½" x 12¼"
30 Bottom Bureau Door Rails (2)	¾" x 2½" x 12¼"
31 Bureau Door Stiles (4)	¾" x 2½" x 18¼"
32 Bureau Door Panels (2)	½" x 12¼" x 14⅛"
33 Fall Front Stiles (2)	¾" x 2½" x 7"

	T x W x L
34 Fall Front Rails (2)	¾" x 2½" x 33"
35 Fall Front Panel (1)	½" x 7" x 27¼"
36 Crown Backer (1)	¾" x 2" x 33"
37 Large Chamfered Molding (1)	¾" x 2" x 63"
38 Bookcase Top Rail (1)	¾" x 2¼" x 33"
39 Small Chamfered Molding (1)	¾" x 1¾" x 58"
40 Square Molding (1)	¾" x ¾" x 58"
41 Bookcase Door Rails (4)	¾" x 2½" x 14½"

Figure 6: *The Roman ogee and the bullnose moldings are cut on the router table. Be sure to sand the top edges of the Roman ogee before installing it.*

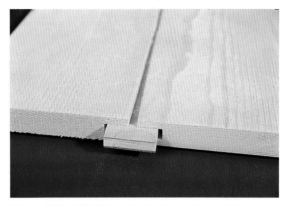

Figure 7: *The ¼"-thick splines in the back are cut from scrap plywood. Solid-wood splines would just crack along their grain.*

very important that the bottom edges of the cleats all line up properly, so draw a pencil line at this location (see the Drawings) all the way around the cupboard to guide you during installation. This line will be hidden by the crown backer (piece 15), which should be installed now. Drive these screws from the inside.

Three moldings are attached to the cleats and backer. The first of these is a large cove molding (piece 16) that is made on your table saw (see cross-section on the Technical Drawings). With the blade lowered below the table, clamp two parallel boards to the saw, as shown in Figure 5, this page.) The boards should be 4" apart and set at a 45° angle to the blade. Your miter gauge can help you set this angle. Test your setup on scrap, making repeated passes

and raising the blade ¹⁄₁₆" after each pass. (Note: For this operation a sharp blade will reduce your sanding time considerably.) When you're satisfied with your test cuts, mill the workpiece.

Make the Roman ogee and bullnose moldings (pieces 17 and 18) on your router table, as shown in Figure 6. Then miter all three moldings to the correct lengths, apply glue on the mitered ends and secure them to the cupboard with finish nails. Set the heads, apply filler and sand smooth.

A Spline-jointed Back

When building cabinets, it can be helpful to attach the back to the carcass as early as possible—a square plywood panel

How to Raise Panels on Your Table Saw

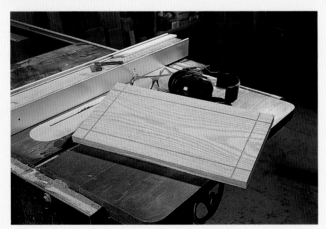

Begin by raising your blade just less than ⅛" above the table, and set the fence 1⅝" from the blade. Use this setup to score the front face of each door four times to create the panel's shoulders (see photo, above). After making these cuts, raise the blade a hair and recut these kerfs for nice clean grooves that will require very little sanding.

Place the panel on edge, then set the blade at 12° and raise it until the teeth meet the shoulder kerfs. Set the fence ¼" from the inside edge of the blade and cut across the grain first, then with it (see photo, above). Keep the panel tight against the fence while you're making these cuts. Now nudge the fence ¹⁄₃₂" closer to the blade and repeat this process to create cleaner bevels.

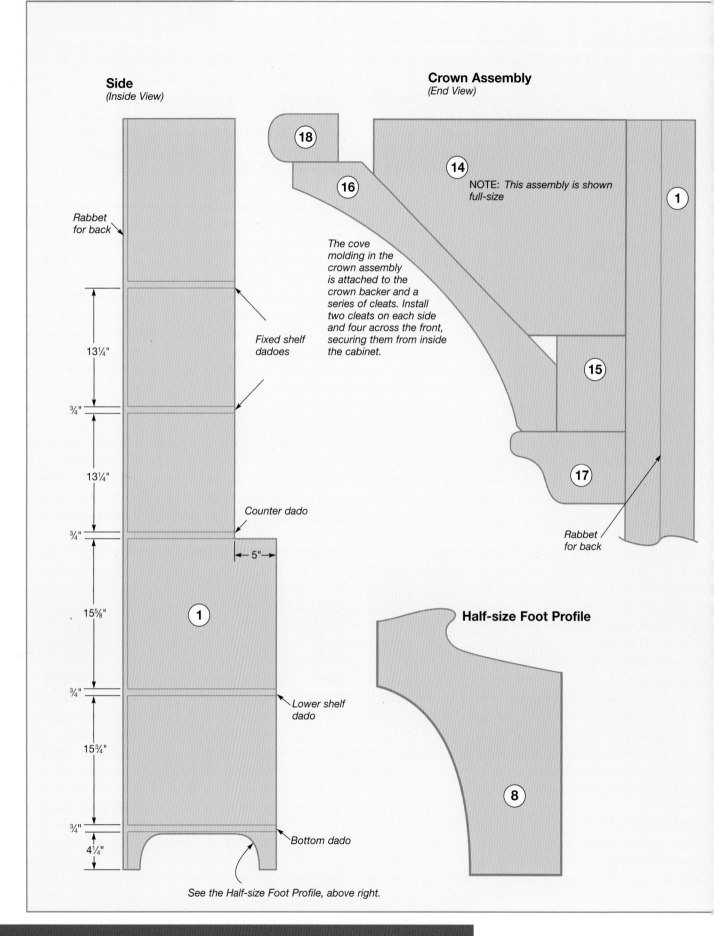

Side
(Inside View)

Crown Assembly
(End View)

NOTE: *This assembly is shown full-size*

Rabbet for back

Fixed shelf dadoes

The cove molding in the crown assembly is attached to the crown backer and a series of cleats. Install two cleats on each side and four across the front, securing them from inside the cabinet.

13¼"

¾"

13¼"

¾"

Counter dado

5"

15⅝"

Rabbet for back

Half-size Foot Profile

¾"

Lower shelf dado

15¾"

¾"

Bottom dado

4¼"

See the Half-size Foot Profile, above right.

Raised Panel Door
(Front View)

When cutting parts for the door, note that the top and bottom rails are not the same widths.

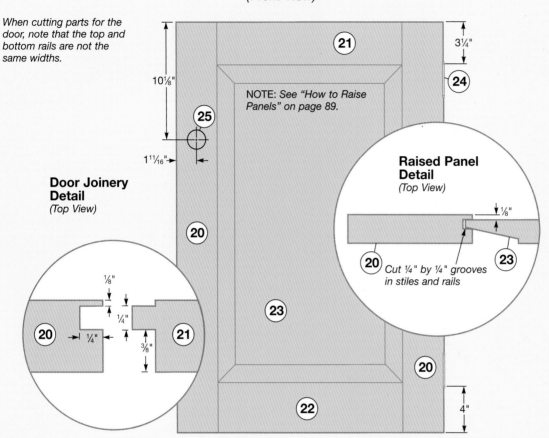

(21)

3¼"

(24)

10⅛"

(25)

NOTE: *See "How to Raise Panels" on page 89.*

1¹¹⁄₁₆"

(20)

(23)

(22)

4"

Raised Panel Detail
(Top View)

⅛"

(20) *Cut ¼" by ¼" grooves in stiles and rails*

(23)

(20)

Door Joinery Detail
(Top View)

⅛"

¼"

(20) ¼" ⅜" (21)

Back Boards and Spline
(Top View)

(2)

(3)

(2)

¼"

⅜"

Fixed Shelves and Counter
(End View)

Use a V-groove bit to make the plate grooves.

2⅛"

(5) (6)

All-Natural Milk Paint

by Larry Fiscus

During the past couple of decades I've driven through most of the contiguous 48 states. Like any traveler, I revel in the drama of great treasures like Yellowstone and the Grand Canyon, but I have to admit that some of my best trips have been simple drives through the pastoral hills of New England and the plains of the Midwest. And my most enduring memories of both regions are of huge red gambrel-roofed barns that dominate every dairy farm.

Have you ever wondered why, with so many color options available, almost every barn in America was painted red? The answer is simple but economically sound: Until the latter half of this century, farmers used their own abundant product—milk—to make the paint they used to spruce up their barns. The formula, developed in Egypt and China a couple of milennia ago, has been used successively through the ages by, among others, Greeks, Romans, and Celts.

There are countless variations on the basic recipes, but the two I've used are listed below. One is for interior projects such as furniture and wainscoting, and the other is for exterior structures such as barns, chicken coops and granaries. Both use the same elements, differing only in the proportions required (by the way, milk paint contains no lead, propellants or other harmful chemicals). With the ingredients in hand, add the milk to the lime, then stir in the linseed oil. Sift the whiting onto the top and let it sink, then stir vigorously with a stick.

The small packages of pigment sold at hardware stores to color cement will work as a coloring agent, as their chemical content is compatible with lime. Mix them with a little water to make a paste, then stir them into the paint.

Experiment with some of your batch to get the color just right, keeping in mind that your paint will be a lot lighter by the time it's finished drying. Then apply it with a bristle or foam brush.

helps keep the cabinet stiff. But the style of this piece predates plywood, so that's not really an option here. Instead, the fixed shelves serve to stiffen the cabinet until you install the three separate boards for the back. The two outside boards have a groove cut along their inside edges, and the center board has the same groove cut into both edges. Refer to the Technical Drawings on pages 90 and 91 for the dimensions, then plow these grooves on the table saw with the workpiece on edge. Use plywood for the splines because solid wood will crack along its grain. Be aware that most ¼" plywood is actually a little thinner, so adjust your groove accordingly. Dry-fit the splines (see Figure 7) and the boards for a snug fit.

Picking up on a colonial theme, the edges of the boards are chamfered where they meet, creating a V. Cut these chamfers with the same V-groove router bit you used earlier to make the shelf plate grooves and be sure to test your setup on scrap before milling the workpieces.

Dry-fit the boards against the carcass and mark the shelf locations, then remove them and use your marks to predrill from the inside for the screws. Countersink the screw holes from the outside and screw the back in place. To allow for expansion and contraction, don't glue the boards or the splines. Drive a tack through each spline near the bottom to stop it from sliding out. Tack the two outside boards to the carcass sides. Attach the glides (pieces 19) next.

Interior Milk Paint
Makes approximately 1 gal.
8 lbs. skim milk
8 oz. linseed oil
2 oz. slaked lime (garden lime)
2 lbs. calcium carbonate (whiting)

Exterior Milk Paint
Makes approximately 1 gal.
8 lbs. skim milk
16 oz. linseed oil
16 oz. slaked lime
6 lbs. whiting